Gina Davidson writes by default. She went to art school and music college under the misguided impressions that she was a) artistic and b) musical, then to teachers' training college in a desperate bid to qualify herself for adult life. Dogged by boredom, she perceived herself as a late developer and went to London University as a mature student where she gained an MA in eighteenth-century English. Her attempts at short story writing and journalism have been acclaimed for their dark humour and eccentric charm and her reflections on motherhood have been recorded in the pages of the *Guardian* and read on Radio 4. She lives in North London with her teenaged daughter and a boxer bitch called Poppy.

WHAT TREASURE DID NEXT

GINA DAVIDSON

A *Virago* Book

First published by Virago in 1996

Copyright © Gina Davidson 1996
Copyright © for illustrations Christine Roche 1996

The moral right of the author has been asserted.

A CIP catalogue record for this book
is available from the British Library.

ISBN 1 86049 114 6

Typeset in New Century Schoolbook by
Palimpsest Book Production Limited,
Polmont, Stirlingshire.
Printed and bound in Great Britain by
Clays Ltd, St Ives plc.

Virago
A Division of
Little, Brown and Company (UK)
Brettenham House
Lancaster Place
London WC2E 7EN

For Amy,
with lots of love

Treasure could shop for hours, even
days without food or rest.

Contents

x

Secrets

Treasure is now nearly fifteen and becoming rather secretive. She has several new pastimes which she is not keen to share with her mother. She will now only talk to her friends behind closed doors or in whispers, has a permanently hunted look and warns friends of my approach with a fearsome grimace. Our home is Moscow pre-glasnost.

I must say this behaviour makes me rather suspicious. Treasure must be up to no good. I become nosier by the day. The Treasure's every move seems suspect. Even pleasant behaviour seems to be part of the plot – a ploy to put me off my guard. It usually precedes a demand: 'Can I have a lift/ more money/ a pizza/ new trainers?'

Momentarily forgetting the tense state of play in our home and because the sun is shining, I ask Treasure whether she and Rosie fancy a walk on the Heath with the dog and me, then perhaps capuccinos and croissants in a café.

'Erk. No thank you,' snarls Treasure. And then her face

brightens. She casts a sly look at Rosie. 'Oh yes, *we'll* take the dog for a walk.'

But it can't be just my absence that makes the prospect attractive. Treasure has chums near the Heath. Boys. Perhaps she is contemplating an hour or so in their company. The dog will be dragged into a den of iniquity and have no excercise.

On the alert for tricks of this sort, I offer to drive Treasure and Rosie to the Heath. Treasure spots Boys on the way. 'Stop,' she shouts. 'There's Andrew and Tony. They can come too. Let us out here.'

We stop only yards from the Heath, but will the Treasure go there? I lurk in the car. Treasure and her chums remain where they are. The dog must be bored to death. We all keep watch, no one goes anywhere. Why? Why doesn't Treasure just proceed to the Heath?

I drive cunningly round the block and spot the little toads again. They have turned back *away* from the Heath. Staggered by Treasure's mendacity I roar up to her little group and shout coarsely from the car window. 'Where are you going? Either take the dog to the bloody Heath or come home.'

Treasure looks shocked to the marrow. How could I speak so crudely in front of her friends and how could I doubt her? She swears on her life that she was going to the Heath.

'You were going the *wrong way*.' I fling the car door open. The dog springs into the back seat and huddles in the corner. It is desperate to be back with its Mummy.

'You are over-reacting,' says Treasure snootily. 'Tony was just going to get his coat.' She is a superior being.

She rolls her eyes and has a whisper. The boys scuttle away. Treasure and Rosie drag the dog out of the car again and off for its walkie. It looks fearfully depressed.

And there's another worry for me. Will Treasure pay attention to the dog? Will she leave it dangling from the jaws of a Rottweiler and skip off for a chat with Boys? And will she pick its poos up like I do? It is a simple procedure with a plastic bag, and as Treasure vows that she loves the dog and is mature enough to handle it, can she deal with its less attractive qualities?' Probably not.

Then I remember that the dog will most likely take charge. It is most responsible. It never argues with Rottweilers, is devoted to Treasure and follows her like a shadow. If only it could speak and report back on her activities, it could infiltrate Treasure's revolutionary cell. I am considering bugging it.

Even this device would provide only a fraction of the information I need. Treasure is rarely accompanied by the dog. She frequents the sort of venue that a sensible dog would never dare approach. I know little of these places. Treasure is unwilling to describe them in depth but occasionally drops the odd terrifying fragment of information: 'The boy next to me got arrested for smoking a spliff./ Rosie fell over dancing and nearly got trampled./ Andrew got mugged on the way home./ Everyone in the squat got raided.'

I feel that the Treasure's reports are heavily censored. It is difficult when mulling over one's child's late night outings, not to let the imagination run riot, through squats, clubs, bedrooms and dark streets.

*   *   *

3

Treasure is also becoming increasingly vague about her whereabouts. Her arrangements are all rather spur of the moment. Tonight she is meeting Delilah at Camden Town, then they're going to meet Andrew at So-and-so's house, and he knows where Chloe's party is, then they're going to it. As soon as she gets there she'll ring and tell me, promise.

'Where, roughly, is Chloe's party?'

'Don't know,' says Treasure in a carefree way. 'But it's in a posh hotel and her parents will be there, then I'm staying the night at her house.'

'Well what's Andrew's friend's address?'

'Don't know,' says Treasure. 'I'm going to phone him and find out.' She rings Chloe again to check the non-arrangements.

'Have you got the address now?'

'She offered to give it me,' says Treasure, still in a buoyant mood, 'but I said I was in a hurry. Anyway, I might see her on the way.'

Chloe too will be travelling through Camden Town where all evenings start. Somehow, among the usual throng of raggedy, dubious and unaccomodated persons that clog this dismal rendezvous, Treasure feels confident that she may spot Chloe as she speeds past in a car to the mystery party address.

I discuss the vagaries of Treasure's arrangements with Mrs B, whose son also goes frequently to Camden Town. They all go there, says she. They mill about, a sort of living fungus around the station and then, from within this mass, up sprouts perhaps a party invitation, notice of a rave, source of a spliff, and off they go. Or they may

4

just stay there all night, sitting on a wall and dangling their legs, wandering the streets roundabout. Mrs B's son prefers these latter options, observing, while Treasure tends to plunge into the thick of things. Naturally neither can reveal plans to their mothers. They have no plans.

'You don't expect her to tell you what she's doing, do you?' Mrs B has always been a realist. 'Stop worrying,' says she strictly. 'They'll be back. They're together aren't they?'

Treasure and Delilah are back sooner than expected. At 8.30 a.m. they return looking rather haggard. They are in their usual formation – Treasure in front yelling rapid and complex explanations, Delilah behind smiling silently. I find this combination makes me rather uneasy.

'Why are you back so early?'

'We had to leave before lunch,' says Treasure, looking oddly blank. Where can they have been? Soho? An opium den? The criminal underworld? To hell and back? I would love to hear all about it, but Treasure now needs to rest. She goes to bed until Monday.

We saw a charming policeman on Kilroy the other day. He too had a fifteen-year-old daughter, and always made sure she told him where she was going and with whom. His work had taught him that this basic information is absolutely essential when one is on the track of a missing juvenile. I really must remember that.

Smoking

Cigarette smoking is all the rage in our house. Now that most of the world deplores it, Treasure and her friends are keen to be at it all the time, stinking the house out, getting cancer and annoying their mothers. Naturally, I have banned it. I am forever trying to enforce my ban. If I go out into the garden I can see them sitting on Treasure's window sill dangling their ciggies out of the window, just in case I come in the door. But I rarely enter the room. I am deterred by the usual villainous compound of stinks – joss-ticks, spray perfume and blasts of nicotine.

Treasure has lied for months about her smoking. 'It wasn't me,' she shouts from her reeking bedroom. 'It was Delilah.'

Delilah is the best friend and perhaps not the perfect role model for Treasure. She smokes, drinks, raves, never works, rarely sleeps or attends lessons and gets A Star for all examinations. Otherwise she is perfectly charming – calm, quiet, modestly dressed, sharp as a tack and polite at dinner.

'I do not smoke,' she croaks,
in a new rasping tone.

'I didn't do any work,' says she pleasantly, 'until two weeks before exams. Then I just stayed up till four in the morning every night and learnt everything.'

This is an immense relief to the Treasure. She can now relax and diddle her life away until May, smoke constantly, work for two brief but hellish weeks, then pass everything in a jiffy. I would like to put the thumb-screws on Delilah until she changes her story. In her absence I suggest that she is perhaps being tremendously stingy with the truth.

'How *can* you call my friend a liar,' bellows the Treasure. 'She says she didn't work, her Mother says she didn't work, and her teachers say she didn't work, so she DIDN'T WORK.'

'Then perhaps she has a photographic memory, but YOU HAVEN'T.'

Treasure stamps to her room to not work. She is now far too upset to do so. She must try on clothes, apply make-up and dance for hours to calm down.

Entering her room upon some pretext I spot an ashtray brimming with dog-ends. 'Who smoked those?'

'It wasn't me,' lies Treasure brazenly. She has taken to nipping out for ten minute walks and then rushing to the bathroom on her return to clean her teeth. I have seen Delilah and Treasure, with my own eyes, sauntering along the street, fags in hands. Still she denies this vice. 'I do not smoke,' she croaks, in a new rasping tone.

'Why can't you speak properly?'

'I lost my voice shouting on the ANL march,' says she proudly in a hoarse whisper.

8   In her earlier youth the Treasure used to be keen on

health. She begged for free-range eggs, no hamburgers, no alcohol and no smoking. She sneered at adult guests and even threw their cigarettes and lighters out of the window. But now the tables are turned. Her room is an oxygen-free zone, her lungs full of black treacle, her friends welcomed reeking of nicotine, leaving a trail of tell-tale stink up and down the stairs. Asthma reigns.

My advisers are shocked. 'You must forbid smoking in your house,' they say. 'Just tell her that she may not do it.'

I must remember to do that as well.

Our Lodger does not smoke. Neither do his children. When visiting they eat meals politely and do as they are told. Naturally it is difficult for Lodger not to smirk as he observes the Treasure's little habits.

Over the last few months Lodger has become highly sensitive to the faults in our household and tormented by what he regards as a high level of filth. To him, one dog hair on the table is fairly close to a river of open sewage. He can no longer bear to eat a crumb in our kitchen.

Gone are the times when we all ate merrily together. Lodger now often dresses in white and wipes every scrap of crockery that he uses with kitchen towel. This puts me in rather a rebellious mood. I may trim the dog's whiskers and scatter them liberally over the crockery.

We cannot go on like this. But luckily Lodger is now rarely here. He is forever at the home of his beloved, soon to become his new partner. We will all be able to relax and behave badly again with no one watching.

Homework

Every now and again Treasure and I fight almost to the death over homework. The weeks speed by. Treasure idles the days away. She hasn't time for a speck of work and naturally, as the deadline draws near, tension mounts.

'Leave me alone,' screams Treasure. 'I will do it. I'm not going out all next week.'

Next week arrives. It dwindles. Treasure diddles her way through it and I am a prisoner in the house. I must remain here to facilitate the homework – barring the phone, repelling visitors, banning outings, withholding pocket money.

'You are *not* to threaten me with money,' raves Treasure. 'I am DOING IT.'

A telephone call breaks through, she grabs it – her lifeline. It is Delilah. 'She's driving me mad,' hisses Treasure down the phone. 'She's so annoying, she's got no life, she's doing my head in.' Her voice drops to a whisper as the critique of her Mama increases in severity.

Meanwhile the homework has mounted up. Ten tons

of it now awaits her, gradually accumulated during the term and now reaching a peak. No wonder Treasure is loath to confront it. For months she has bluffed her way through life.

'I did it at school,' she has cried gaily. 'I had two free periods.' This frees her to spend her evening busily experimenting with coiffures and reading Virginia Andrews.

Sometimes a space appears in the dense and persistent playtime and a calm hour or so of homework breaks through. For a short while our house is an airy, relaxed place, but then along comes a nasty bit of algebra or some baffling physics or a French verb and Treasure is off again with a shriek. 'I can't do it,' and back to the plaits, outfits and Ambient music. Now here we are, the deadline almost upon us and the battle raging.

'You are obsessed with academic success,' says my Advisor strictly. 'You can't *make* her do it. She must *want* to.'

But why should Treasure want to do it? There are a thousand other things she wants to do more – chat, play, dance about, shop, squeeze the dog. She is not raring to spend a quiet and peaceful day at home alone acquiring knowledge. In order to work she needs loud background noise, a couple of friends lolling about the floor and an interruption at least every fifteen minutes – a snack, a bath, a phone call, a visitor, a row. These things help her to study.

Only one thing wrecks her concentration. Me. The tap of my typewriter, a whispered instruction to the dog, or any hint that she has a living mother in the house, drives the Treasure wild. She throws her work   11 aside and bursts into my room at the first tap or murmur.

'You're doing it on purpose,' she shouts in despair, her ambitions thwarted. 'Why are you doing this to me? I'm trying to write this really difficult essay and you're making a noise all the time. YOU DON'T WANT ME TO WORK.'

The Laundry

Treasure has turned our home into a giant laundry, its radiators perpetually festooned with drying clothes, the washing machine churning night and day, the stairs and chairs piled with ironing. She is forever flinging mounds of clothing at the bathroom clothes basket, selected in a random way from the piles in her room.

'They're all DIRTY,' bellows Treasure, glaring at the latest heap.

How is this possible? They weren't dirty yesterday. In one weekend she has managed to dirty seven T-shirts, four jumpers, three pairs of jeans, one pair of flares, five dresses, three skirts and two nighties. They all look perfectly clean to me.

'How can you have worn all this since Friday?'

'I HAVE,' screeches the Treasure. 'How *can* you call me a liar?'

She has perhaps not quite realised that there is a difference between wearing and trying on. If a garment touches her body for one second, Treasure feels that she

13

'They're all DIRTY,' bellows Treasure, glaring at the
latest heap.

14

has worn it. And as she tries on several dozen outfits a day, then casts them upon the floor, dances on them and forgets them, it is naturally easy to confuse them with the dirty clothes, also on the floor, and with the clean clothes, which have just been delivered to her room by the slave from the downstairs laundry.

I give Treasure a washing-machine lesson so that she may occasionally cope with the continually developing heaps herself. But the machine refuses to co-operate. It perhaps recognises the author of its slavery.

'It won't work,' shouts Treasure, glaring at it. It needs coaxing, its doors need opening and shutting again firmly, its switches must be fiddled with. I explain this to Treasure rather pointlessly. She has glazed over at the first malfunction and can absorb no more information.

Meanwhile, she knows that at her heels the clothing mounds are growing. She has no time to pander to a whimsical machine. She must be up there, hurling more piles at the clothes basket, searching the radiators and clean piles for more garments, carrying them up to the piles in her room and, most tiresome of all, putting the clean items into the drawers and wardrobe and onto the shelves.

It is this final task that stumps her – the sorting, folding, arranging and putting away. It is so time consuming. She procrastinates, and then she is done for, because the dirty pile and the tried-on pile begin to cover the clean pile, and all is confusion again.

Out goes a mélange from the piles, down to the clothes basket once more and into the cleansing circuit. We are both on a treadmill.

15

I ask Treasure whether she could perhaps try to differentiate between the various piles before casting them into the basket, but the glazed look is on her again. She begins to wander from my room roughly two-thirds of the way through my sentence.

'Cool,' says she on her way out. Apparently this word implies that she has assimilated my suggestion, will carry it out and our problem will be solved. I do hope so.

Holidays

Another Summer has arrived, another six-week holiday period for Treasure, and how is she to fill it? She is now fond of luxury and exotic locations. She needs friends, clubs, surfing, a thrilling night-life and boys. I need heat, charming beaches and countryside, and peace and quiet. And the dog has to come. This rather limits our choice.

'We never go anywhere nice,' lies the Treasure. 'Rosie's mum is taking her to Club Med in Tobago. Why can't we go?' But we are constrained by cost and quarantine laws.

We choose Cornwall – a flat in St Ives, minutes from the beach and town centre where five girls and a dog are allowed. And I even have a friend along the coast, should I be driven mad by girls and need a grown-up to talk to. What could go wrong?

Treasure starts packing for this cleverly planned holiday. She discovers a huge snag. Many essential items are hidden beneath the piles of debris in her bedroom. In order to find them she must first clear the piles. This fearful prospect renders her inert. Now and again an odd sleeve or corner of some long forgotten or beloved garment will poke out of a pile. It is rescued, washed, worn briefly and swallowed up again in the wild room.

Once, months ago, Treasure's room was heaven, just after Lodger painted it blue, but gradually the Quatermass of bits grew, a relentlessly increasing mass, out of Treasure's control. And now she is under added pressure. Rosie is coming to stay the night. Treasure desperately needs to clear a space for her visitor.

This morning she opens her eyes to chaos. The Quatermass has grown. Dotted with ancient and wasted glasses of fruit juice bubbling with mould, it is threatening to envelop the bed. Treasure begs for assistance.

'You've got to help me tidy my room. Please will you? Can we do it after school? Please? Before Rosie comes.'

Just for starters I look under the bed and rake out some horrors: a bubbling mould drink, ruined tights, last term's sandwiches, a rather distasteful paperback and a cigarette end. To whom did the last item belong? Treasure has not the faintest idea.

In the afternoon I race home for our tidying appointment. Treasure does not appear. The minutes tick by, forty of them. She has never been this late home from school. When do I phone the police? How late does a child have to be? I am feeling rather cold and sweaty.

Eventually, Treasure wanders in, surprised to find that I am not smiling.

'Where have you BEEN?'

'I've been talking to my friends. I thought you *wanted* me to have friends at school.'

'You're forty minutes late. You're meant to phone and let me know what you're doing.'

'SOR-REE.' Treasure curls her lip. 'All right, *don't* ask me what sort of day I had.'

I don't ask. I have to leave the house shortly, the Quatermass is still festering, Rosie is approaching the front door. Treasure has forgotten her morning's intentions. Upon my return both Treasure and Rosie are relaxing in the tip.

I cast the problem from my mind and concentrate on the kitchen – a second problem area which sprouts mess in a flash. As I toil away, scrubbing, tidying and cooking, I hear an unusual sound from upstairs. It is the roar of the hoover. Then an excited call from Treasure.

'I've done my room. Look at my room.'

I look. Treasure's room is immaculate. At last the piles have gone. 'I did it in fourteen minutes,' says she, prancing across the yards of clear carpet. 'All my dirty clothes are in the bathroom.'

But still she cannot pack. She is now too tired. She cannot pack the next day. She is resting, visiting Chloe, staying the night and the next morning, and working in the afternoon for slave wages at the mini-market. It will then be the eve of our departure. I hear her planning yet another outing on the phone to Rosie.

'We must go somewhere,' she hisses. 'It's our last night of freedom.'

'You must not,' I scream. 'You must PACK.'

'How *dare* you listen to my conversations,' roars the Treasure. 'You're so nosey.'

I forsee an evening of hell tomorrow, packing. To be

19

Her hair is concealed by a towel. She dare not reveal it.
'You'll be cross,' she howls. 'You'll shout.'

20

followed, presumably, by a fortnight of hell on holiday. I have never quite understood why holidays are thought to be relaxing.

Treasure, Rosie, the dog and I arrive at our holiday appartment in Cornwall. The sea-view is delightful, but the furious swirling patterns of the carpet and soft furnishings come as rather a shock. Mr and Mrs Landlord stare at us carefully.

As Treasure and Rosie rush off in search of surfers I mention to Mrs Landlord, in a humorous way, that they wish to sleep on the beach. What does she think? Is it dangerous down here? Are there drugs? Mrs Landlord smiles politely. She wouldn't know about things like that.

Off I go to walk the dog. It has been a gruelling seven-hour drive from London and I am rather looking forward to a relaxing evening. But upon my return I find Mr Landlord in a state of uproar. My casual remark about sleeping on beaches, the mention of drugs and the prospect of three more girls, has terrorised his wife. One brief glimpse of us has given her the terminal vapours. She is desperate for us to leave. In grovelling fashion I promise we will all be good and in by midnight, according to The Rules. No one will sleep on beaches. At last Mr Landlord is pacified. We may stay.

And then Treasure and Rosie return, thrilled with the beach and its inhabitants. This is their favourite resort, Baywatch in English, until they hear about Mr and Mrs Landlords' criticism and curfew. Deeply offended they retire to their room. A peaceful hour passes, then a fierce knocking on our door. It is Mr and Mrs Landlord in a

emper and brandishing a doily. Unknown to me,
e, feeling rebellious, had flung it from the window.
ily is our undoing.

y wife had a premonition,' roars Mr Landlord. 'She
ew something bad would come of this. She is *never*
wrong.'

Loud screams of mocking laughter from Treasure and
Rosie at the top of the stairs prove to Mr Landlord that
his wife was right once again. They are being invaded by
inner-city delinquents. We are ordered to leave at dawn.

Treasure and Rosie are almost delighted. 'It's very
rock-and-roll,' says Rosie.

'What do you mean?'

'Well, rock stars get thrown out of their hotels, don't
they? Axel Rose got thrown out.'

In two days Delilah, Lizzie and Daisy arrive and we will
be homeless – five girls, one demented mother and a dog.
I hurry to the pub for a brandy and telephone, to find us
a home. We are in luck. My friend staying nearby tells us
that there is a heavenly farmhouse available out on the
rugged coast road in a charming village.

We must pack up again quickly. But the dog, a sensitive
creature, has perhaps sensed our distress and peed on
the sofa. It never does this at home. I must wash the
tell-tale patch on the sofa and dry it with the hair
dryer, praying that Mr and Mrs Landlord won't spot it
and demand payment for their ruined furniture. After
only one night our holiday has taken on a nightmare
quality.

We escape and drive through pelting rain to my friend's
holiday home. I have a short weep and tea and toast.

Luckily the new farmhouse is heavenly – spacious, tasteful, secluded and, for one brief hour or so, bathed in sunlight.

We move in. But Treasure is a dab hand at fouling up holidays. Left briefly alone on the surfing beach with Rosie, she quickly squanders all her holiday money on a stylish wet suit and boogie-board.

'It's my money,' she shrieks, unrepentant. 'I can spend it on what I like.' Then suddenly the colour drains from her cheeks. 'Oh God!'

'What's the matter now?'

'You'll go mad. Promise you won't be cross. Promise? I've left my cash card at the other place. It's in my make-up bag in a drawer.'

I must now phone the dreaded Mr and Mrs Landlord again. Yes, they have the bag. On my instructions, Mr Landlord looks inside. Yes, the card is in it. But Treasure had omitted to tell me that the bag also contains a stack of souvenir condoms from the Strobe Aids Awareness Evening. What must Mr Landlord have thought? Treasure assures me that she keeps them for sentimental rather than practical reasons.

Thank goodness no one in the new village yet knows that we are outcasts. Our reputation is unsullied. Until Treasure visits the pub with Rosie and, fond of a chat, tells the locals our story. By chance our new landlord is among them. Will we be hounded out again?

Treasure and her friends are an exhuberant bunch. To this quiet corner of Cornwall they have brought the flavour of Holloway. Pop music booms from their bedrooms, the

23

television roars, the lights blare, the meter runs out. The bathroom is in constant use and the hair-dryer whirrs forever. The picturesque floorboards of our farmhouse resound with the clumping of Doc Martens and clogs and the peaceful village air is rent with squeals.

Down here Treasure's urban language rather grates on the sensibilities. The word 'horny' is in constant use. I am assured that this now merely means an attractive male. It is applied to the surf-board and wet-suit vendor and some of his chums. Treasure and Rosie are apt to call it out of the car window at passing youths, considerably lowering the tone of our group, I feel.

The dog has taken to hiding under the kitchen table. Its nerves are in shreds and so are mine. We wander the cliff tops together, breathing deeply and trying to regain our composure. I am fearful that the villagers may rebel *en masse* and cast us out, just as Mr and Mrs Landlord did. But luckily our farmhouse is set back from the village and slightly isolated, and the squealing somewhat muffled by the constant mist and rain. I transport the girls to the surfing beach as often as possible, where they may shriek freely.

But multiple periods and wretched dull weather have rather put paid to the surfing. No one seems to mind very much. Treasure and her friends are keen on sitting about. They sit on the beach, in the beach café, on the harbour wall, outside the Tate. I cannot induce them to look inside the Gallery. My suggestion of a bracing walk along the coastal path has been ignored. All five treasures prefer to rest until midday, aiming to leave the house at 2 p.m. They have shown interest only in a disco and local cider and wine farm where free tasting is encouraged.

Luckily my friend Mrs H is staying up the road. I have a grown-up to talk to. In her house the silence is almost absolute. Her son reads quietly and together they visit churches and exhibitions, chatting in a cultivated way, taking healthy walks and swims. Mrs H is loving her holiday. She appreciates the scenery, the solitude, that Katherine Mansfield stayed next door and D.H. Lawrence lived round the corner.

Inspired by her example I again suggest to the girls that we all visit the Tate. There is little response. I will treat them. Still no response. Treasure has other more pressing plans.

'I've got to Sun-In my hair tomorrow,' says she. 'We've been planning it for ages.'

This means another day of intensive showering, hair-drying and clomping. Eventually she swans into the kitchen, her hair the colour of a banana. Hair slightly lightened by the sun and a healthy complexion would have been my choice, but there is no sun and Treasure never was one for moderation.

She has, however, helped with the cooking, assuming the role of head prefect and becoming rather authori-tative. We have had cream teas, crab, fresh mackerel, picnics and non-stop catering. Our holiday is almost at an end. I have a final stab at mustering up enthusi-asm for the Tate. The girls agree to go. They seem almost keen. Perhaps the countryside has had a slightly beneficial effect after all. I am exhausted but have a sense of achievement. I have endured a week with five girls without a major row or tragedy. I now need a holiday.

On our last afternoon I find Daisy making a large sandwich in the kitchen. 'It's so relaxing here,' says she dreamily. 'I could stay forever.'

We return to an empty house. Our Lodger has finally gone. He is to live with his beloved in a small but rather chic flat in Docklands. Only his fax and telephone remain for a few fleeting days. But he has left his mark – a mountain of sawdust in the garden, chasms in the plaster where his burglar alarm wire used to lie, a felt carpet of dust on all shelves.

'Disgraceful,' says my neighbour Mrs Perez. 'I wouldn't let him get away with that.' But I will. Another con-tretemps seems pointless. Lodger and I were creepily pleasant to each other over the last few months of his stay, pretending to be friends.

Treasure, in an annoying way, sticks up for Lodger through thick and thin. 'Lodger's cocked up the hoover,' says she with a proud smirk.

'I'm not very pleased with him,' say I, rather moder-ately, I feel, but Treasure sides with the enemy.

'Why are you so nasty about him? You're always nasty.'

To Treasure, Lodger has recently become a rather Christlike figure, unjustly persecuted by her evil mother. As I scrape away at the filth left behind on his bathroom floor, I wonder why. She is desolate at his departure after five years. I am not. Neither is the dog. It will no longer have to endure Lodger's baiting and slaps disguised as robust pats. The dog and I share a celebratory fig-roll.

26

Now that Lodger has left I realise the meaning of 'undermining'. Lodger was forever doing it. Using a continual flow of criticism disguised as jokes, he established an uneasy feeling in the Treasure's mind that her mother was untidy, too fond of the dog and generally inadequate.

These critiques are based on truth but it was not helpful of Lodger to highlight them. It has not aided me in my battle to be an effective Mummy.

A Hairstyle for the Holiday

Back home again I call Treasure for dinner.

'It'll have to wait ten minutes,' she barks crossly. She is up to something complex in the bathroom and is tremendously harassed. At last she appears, her hair wrapped modishly in a plastic bag. Not satisfied with the banana colour achieved on holiday, she wishes to be even blonder. The Sun-In on holiday was not enough. I question Treasure about the product she has applied to her hair. Her answers are rather vague.

Throughout the evening I sporadically beg Treasure to take the plastic bag off her head. She refuses. The hours pass by. It is 11.30 – my bedtime.

'I'm not tired at all,' says Treasure, bouncing around with the bag on. 'I'm wide awake. I'm going to wash it off now.' She has again forgotten that midnight hair-washing is a sure-fire method of enraging her mother.

'Dry it downstairs,' I shout, stamping off to bed. 'I don't want to hear you.'

But I do hear her. In half an hour there is a strange whimpering noise outside my door. It is Treasure, traumatised. The alarming result of her hairdressing has made her ill with shock.

'I've got asthma,' says she, clutching her throat. Her face crumples, she begins to cry bitterly. Her hair is concealed by a towel. She dare not reveal it. 'You'll be cross,' she howls. 'You'll shout.'

I swear to do neither. Treasure allows a fraction of the hair to show. It is acrylic primrose after several years of drought.

'Is it horrible?'

'No,' I lie. There is her face, red from crying, surrounded by the yellow remains of her hair. A desolate sight. Further criticism would be uncalled for. 'Doesn't matter,' I say. 'It's not too bad. How long were you meant to leave it on for?'

'Two hours,' says she, studying the leaflet. I remind her that she left it on for five. She is never keen on reading instructions in advance. It takes too long, and once embarked on a project she is dead keen to get on with it in a spontaneous way, improvising freely. A vicious peroxide does not respond well to this approach.

Too late, Treasure and I pore over the instructions. This was rather a sly product. Treasure had in fact used only the first part of it. The glaring yellow is a half-way stage. Having removed every trace of natural colour, she must now purchase the second part to replace some. And quickly. Only one day to go before she goes off on an activity holiday, and should she enter the swimming pool, her hair, if only semi-treated, may turn green.

Thoughtless criticism and cries of horror from friends

29

and neighbours increase the pressure. We rush out to buy the second half of this nightmare product, scouring the chemists of North London. No one has heard of it. At last we find some. Together we study the instructions assiduously. They are imprecise. This stage is obviously a casual affair. With little guidance, Treasure and I smear on ruinous solution number two. We have a tense time spotting pale patches and achieving uniform smearing.

We wash it off exactly on time. This potion slightly dulls the glaring yellow. Treasure leaves for her holiday looking slightly more subtle. But will she be tempted to tamper with herself further while away from her mother? Perhaps a crew cut and nose jewelry are on the cards.

It is perhaps a good idea for Treasure and I to have a short holiday apart. Then I can have my ideal holiday – one week alone with the dog in complete silence, no futile preparation of meals for Treasure to waste or ignore or allow to cool and congeal. No bickering, just the odd bark.

But Treasure rings after only two days of Activity Holiday. Please, please can she come home? She is miserable as sin.

'They're so strict,' says she in a heart-rending way, 'and it's so cold at night and the beds are so uncomfortable and I'm not allowed in Chloe's dormitory and anyway she's going home next week and everybody else here is TEN and I'll be by myself with JUNIORS. And I want to be with YOU,' she wails. 'Next year I want to go away with YOU.'

My heart warms tremendously to Treasure as she makes this declaration. I cannot bear her to suffer the harsh regime of the Activity Holiday. I mention her request to some of my Advisors.

'Make her stay,' they all shout with one accord. 'I hope you weren't thinking of letting her come home! She'll never stick at anything.' They are horrified at my weediness.

I ring the heartless leaders of the Activity Holiday to ask about Treasure's incarceration and welfare.

'She's fine,' says the gentleman in charge reassuringly. For the first few days his office is often clogged with weeping girls, waiting for their mothers to phone. 'Don't worry,' says he. 'Things will improve.'

Sure enough, they do. I soon receive a charming letter from Treasure begging to stay an extra week. She describes the jet-ski instructor in glowing terms. Please can she have more pocket money to go jet-skiing again? And can she have more socks, writing paper, stamps, batteries for her camera and, something of a surprise, her French homework? I am charmed by this final request and send all items demanded.

I ring to check that the parcel has arrived. Yes. And Treasure has been camping out for the night, says my Informant. She has put up her own tent. Not a scrap of food was allowed until she had done so. Treasure was apparently particularly adept at whacking in stakes with a mallet.

It is difficult for me to imagine the Treasure in such a situation: outdoors, independent, healthy, energetic and good-humoured. As I had hoped, this holiday is a sort of respite care for both of us.

I hear little from Treasure over the next week, just the

odd reverse charge phone call at peak time from Cumbria, begging for more pocket money. And in no time at all her holiday is over. There she is descending from the coach, smiling and waving happily.

But as she draws near I see that the smile is a brave cover-up. She is in fact surrounded by Gestapo. She whispers a dreadful warning.

'You won't *believe* what happened,' she hisses. 'We nearly called the police. Wait here. I've got to say goodbye.' Fearlessly she darts back to her friends, then back again. 'Mr X *hit* me,' she whispers fiercely. 'Would you believe it? He pushed me over.'

Safely in our getaway car she is at last able to speak freely of her ordeal. Something like pindown seems to have been employed to restrain Treasure and her chums over the final days. Expulsion was threatened, great cruelty employed. 'We had to *work* for them. We had to work all day in the tuck shop, then they locked us up in separate rooms at night and I wasn't allowed to speak to this boy and Lola was going to phone the police and I was hysterical.'

'Sounds terrible. Did you do anything dreadful to make them so cross?' I enquire in a light and pleasant manner so as not to inhibit Treasure.

'We didn't *do* anything. We were just noisy all the time,' says she airily. '*They* were disgusting and they're going to write to you and complain and we're never allowed to go there again and I bought you this special present and it got nicked.'

'So it was horrid was it? The last week?'

'No,' says Treasure. 'It was great. I loved it.'

Boyfriends

Now that all our holidays are over the sun has come out. I rush into the garden in my chic new bikini. Treasure is horrified. 'Oh my God, what's that? It doesn't fit. Look. There's all fat hanging out.'

Treasure indicates the hip area. Perhaps the Cornish cream teas have taken their toll. 'Pull the bottom up,' she commands. Bravely overcoming her revulsion, she wrenches at the costume, desperate to improve my appearance. 'It's no good. It looks disgusting. Fancy paying all that money for something that doesn't fit!'

'Just forget my costume and show me the French homework.' Months and months have elapsed and still Treasure cannot master the verb 'to be'. This is ruining her chances of ever coming to grips with the perfect tense. Our plan was to practise verbs in the sunny garden, but Treasure is at once distracted by my ill-fitting bikini.

It is not difficult to distract the Treasure from her studies. Anything can do it: a garment, a breeze, the dog, my costume, the phone of course, but most of all, a

33

boy – the thought of a boy, a glimpse of one, the mention of, the prospect, the idea of a boy. The verb *être* hasn't a chance in hell of retaining Treasure's attention.

Driving along the other day with Treasure and Rosie, both more or less somnolent, Rosie spotted a car. It contained two boys. 'Look,' she shrieked, 'it's those boys from Andrew's party, in a *Beetle*.' Both girls sprang to life, riveted to the subject. The verb *être* would be jealous as anything.

'Oh my God,' Treasure was faint with excitement. 'They're just behind us. Can you believe it?' For miles the girls chattered about this sighting. Crabby and embittered by a trail of faulty relationships, I am wearied by this ceaseless enthusiasm for chaps.

'Did I behave like this in my youth?' I ask Mrs B. 'I can't remember.' I vaguely recall painting flames on a biker's helmet in an adoring way, but I was also a swot at school, poring avidly over verbs.

'Course you did,' snaps Mrs B briskly. 'Everyone does. It's a wonder any girl ever passes an exam.'

Can these fellows be worthy of such attention? They often come into our house and skulk into Treasure's room or slouch about the kitchen. They barely speak, sometimes even refusing food, and depart without a word of farewell, leaving empty beer cans and cigarette ends behind them. Treasure's room becomes malodorous.

Yesterday a rather sullen pair turned up. 'They're very nice boys,' Treasure told me. 'Sometimes David is a bit rude, but Peter is really nice.'

This description was wildly off the mark. They were laden with drink and cigarettes and did not speak in my presence. I banned them fom visiting the next day, not wishing our home to become known as a dive in which minors may drink and smoke freely. And they were sabotaging Treasure's French.

But suddenly I realise that boys may be used to encourage learning. Before any encounter with or outing involving boys, Treasure must learn one verb and one chunk of vocabulary. 'No French,' say I callously, 'no Strobe/Ritzy/Market/Andrew's house.' How odd that I never thought of this before.

Treasure rushes to the downstairs phone. Her voice sinks to a whisper. 'She's gone completely mad. She's making me do this French. She's pathetic. She's really pathetic.'

Meanwhile, Treasure's French is coming on apace, so I shall stick at it. I feel that we have little time left for verbs. Thoughts of boys increasingly preoccupy the Treasure and soon her every waking moment will be swamped by Romance. Boys are the world's greatest distraction and what bad luck that they coincide with GCSEs.

And now we have another distraction. Selina the charming new lodger has arrived – a young costume designer. Just right for Treasure. She now has someone pleasant in the house to talk to about clothes, pop music, shopping, modelling, broken hearts and boys. Bliss. She obviously cannot discuss these topics with her dull and ignorant mother. And Selina is forever cooking pasta with exotic sauces featuring sherry and cream, *and* she has an artist boyfriend with a pony-tail. We live Mills and Boon.

Suddenly our house is more thrilling. It is full of youth and style rather than just a lumbering old mother and occasionally Grandma plodding about downstairs on another planet. Artists and film persons visit, rush up the stairs, drink wine and play pop music. Our home is a youth club. As the weeks pass my longing to live alone in an isolated cave increases, but the Treasure is in heaven.

Soon she has dragged up the ghastly subject of Boys in the Bedroom again. 'Why can't Andrew sleep in my bedroom?' she shouts. 'Why not?'

'Because this is my house and I say so.' My Advisors have told me that this is an adequate answer. Treasure does not agree with them.

'Stop saying that,' she screams. 'Just tell me why. What do you think I'll do?'

'Probably nothing, but you are not having boys in your room overnight.'

Treasure is beside herself. 'You're not answering me properly. Just *answer me. Why not?*'

'Because I say so.' Treasure is most dissatisfied. She stamps up and down the living room roaring. I expect a complaint from neighbours at any moment. But suddenly the Treasure stops screeching. She has had a sly thought.

'But I can have them in my room in the evening, can't I?'

'Yes.'

'Well I could be *doing it* in the evening, couldn't I? So what's the difference?' Treasure glares triumphantly. She is on to a winner here, but still I cling to my apparently insane ruling.

'You are not even fifteen and may not have boys in your room overnight.'

Treasure tends to disregard such instructions. She likes to go on asking the same question repeatedly until the instructor, maddened by hours of ceaseless repetition, weakens under the strain and comes up with a new and more pleasing answer. 'But why can't Andrew stay?' she yells on. 'He's not my *boyfriend*. WHY NOT?'

'You can never tell what will happen.'

'What?' Treasure's jaw drops open. She knows now that she is addressing a worm with a sewer for a brain. Fighting to overcome her distaste, she continues her questioning. 'I don't know what will happen?' She raises her eyes to heaven. 'I see. I don't know what will happen.' She cannot avoid heavy sarcasm. She is a sage talking to a woman who has not lived. Sickened, she leaves the room.

Ruthlessly I stick to my ruling. Terrifying reports have been flooding in which strengthen my resolve. Mrs A has told me dreadful stories of goings on in girls' bedrooms overnight, reported to her by her frank and upright daughter. Strange new terminology is now used that Mrs A and I have never heard before and which is much too vile to print. And Mrs C tried to be forthright with her daughter the other day going along in the car.

'Look Jennifer,' said she, 'You're only thirteen and I don't want you even thinking about boyfriends for years.'

'You don't know what I've done already,' said Jennifer, in a rather sneering way from the back of the car. Mrs C slammed on the brakes, narrowly avoiding a mammoth pile-up in the High Street.

'You're making it up,' she screamed, but Jennifer just went on smirking and lolling quietly in the back seat. Mrs C was terribly shaken. Her daughter is tall, blond and beautiful. People gape as she walks by, men circle around her on beaches.

Meanwhile the Treasure nags on. She resumes nagging at tea-time. She will nag until I drop. Oh for a daughter who likes to stay in practising the piano and goes horse riding at weekends. That's what I used to do.

But Treasure has a burning ambition not to grow up like her mother. She is eager to rip out all the relevant chromozomes and burn them. She receives the odd bit of encouragement from chums.

'If your mother likes him you'd better get rid of him,' said Lizzie grumpily the other day, about Michael Billings, a pleasant fellow that Treasure has recently chummed up with. If she must have a boyfriend, then this one would be perfect.

I also receive supportive advice. 'Try some paradoxical injunction,' says Mrs Perez. 'Someone's written a book on it.' She suggests that I scowl at Treasure's pleasant chums and smile charmingly at the ill-mannered skulkers. Can I do it? It's probably too late anyway.

Selina our new lodger was chatting to Treasure yesterday. 'Do you have any ambitions?' she asked, truthfully interested.

'I want to live in a squat in Finsbury Park,' said Treasure flippantly. It is Culture that she is fiercely opposed to at present. At the sound of Radio 3 her mood darkens. The words 'classic' and 'theatre' throw her into sullen rebellion.

We were all chatting politely about such things at dinner on Saturday. There we were sitting properly at table with our roast, gravy, three veg and serviettes – Treasure, Michael Billings, Selina, Gardener and I. We'd all been out and about sopping up culture over the last year or so, except for Treasure. She was unable to sit patiently absorbing knowledge, but preferred to pepper the conversation with barbed and offensive comments.

'I'd rather go down the Strobe and in the chippy,' said she in a fiercely yobby tone, and gollupped her dinner down in a trice.

The polite conversation had been rather a shock to her system and she fought bravely and independently to put a stop to it. 'It's traditional to fight at dinner in this house,' she explained to the boyfriend with a knowing smirk.

An accurate observation. Our dinner table is usually a battlefield. Treasure, the dinner and I are the casualties, the dog the only beneficiary. It receives the regular ruins of our meals.

I reprimand Treasure rather harshly the next day about her behaviour at table. She is most surprised.

'I wasn't rude,' she shouts. 'I was *not rude*.' She looks suddenly wretched. She felt left out, she explains. She was only being rude about herself. She didn't know anything about things like that and nobody asked *her* what *she'd* been doing.

Possibly my attempts at cultural outings with Treasure have lacked enthusiasm. My Advisors often suggest that I spend more of the right sort of time with Treasure. What

39

do they mean? I try again. A fresh start is perhaps in order. I invite Treasure to the cinema. She may like to see *Much Ado*, just like Rosie and her mother did in a harmonious way.

Treasure selects *The Fugitive* instead. She seems to rather enjoy it. She guzzles popcorn and chocolate, she chatters all the way home, she enters the house. And then she remembers her ambition. She is desperate to go out at once despite the lateness of the hour.

'I've got to see someone else,' she wails. 'I just want to go next door to see Jane. I've been with you for TWO HOURS.'

She is at risk of personality infection.

Sadly we see little more of Michael Billings. I am most disappointed. But the serious quest for a boyfriend has obviously begun. To Treasure and her chums a boyfriend is a form of life support. No girl can live without one. Decades of feminism have done nothing for them.

Treasure also longs for me to find romance.

'Why don't you marry him?' she nags, referring to some old acquaintance of mine who dropped by. And she considers the Gardener a possibility. Not only does she long to be a bridesmaid, but she is also keen to get her mother off her back. 'Then you'll have something else to think about except me.'

Unfortunately, Treasure seems to be developing a penchant for bad boys, the sort that go late night raving, have rows with their mothers and hanker after noise, drugs and other women. This search is taking up much of the Treasure's life. What's more it has nothing to do with her mother. Obviously. A mother knows nothing of romance and sex and does not have boyfriends. Treasure is not always keen for me to have a boyfriend. She goes off the idea as soon as it happens. She wavers and gets browned off with the Gardener, now that he has begun to hang around after gardening and stay to dinner.

'Is he your boyfriend?' she asks with a gimlet sneer.

'Don't be silly.'

'He is, isn't he? Isn't he? He's so boring. Why is he always here? Hasn't he got a home to go to?' Knowing that Gardener is within earshot, Treasure speaks loudly and clearly. With any luck, this will scare him off, if he is a boyfriend.

Then she wavers again. She cannot make her mind up. A glamourous mother with a boyfriend is better than a drudge mother with a dog. Everyone else's mother has a boyfriend or a husband.

'Rosie's mother's getting married,' says Treasure wistfully. 'He's ever so nice. Why can't you? Then I can be bridesmaid.' This would mean a snazzy new dress. She is even prepared to be pleasant occasionally to the Gardener. 'Go on. Please.' She nags on. 'Then you won't just have me to think about all the time.'

For fifteen years I have had no one else to worry about. This has been a tremendous burden for the Treasure, but she can do nothing to lighten it. Her pastimes are becoming more worrying as she grows up – the clubs wilder, the nights later, the outfits more *risqué*, the friends more dubious and the exams closer.

If only her mother had a stable relationship with a chap, things might calm down. Or would they?

Treasure's Anxieties

Treasure and I have a pleasant morning shopping, her favourite pastime. We go wild in Marks and Spencers and Rymans replenishing our supply of knickers, tights, pens, cartridges and all beginning of term requirements. Even Treasure is staggered at the cost. 'Let's get out of here,' says she hoarsely, 'before we see anything else.' A harmonious morning.

Back at home Treasure rushes to complete some GCSE coursework – Media Studies one year in advance. She is a model child. Thinking we are in for a quiet afternoon I ring Mrs B. But Treasure can sense a phone-call from miles away. She bursts in, white-faced and tense. 'Will you please come and help me,' she snaps.

'I'm on the phone.' Treasure retreats. Seconds later she returns.

'How long will you be?' An eruption seems imminent. Mrs B is keen to discuss an urgent problem. Treasure is about to blow. Resolutely I continue with my phone-call. Treasure whirls in and out, roaring and stamping. At the

42

other end of the phone Mrs B is shocked to the marrow by these interruptions. In comes Treasure again, fists clenched, face puce, molten lava on the way.

'I've got to get to the shops. I NEED things. The shops will CLOSE.' She is weeping with desperation.

I often find myself in this position – a distraught person at one end of the phone and Treasure screaming at the other. Whichever one I deal with my conversation is stymied. This is always a sudden event, I cannot prepare myself. One minute Treasure is quietly composed, the next she is in turmoil.

'Shut your door,' says Mrs B horrified, but what is a door to the Treasure in her present condition? It bursts open, in she roars again, ripping the telephone from its socket. She screams on. 'Other parents help their children. They come in and say, 'How are you getting on? Can I help you?' But YOU DON'T.'

Perhaps Treasure is right. I hear that libraries all over England are full of parents doing their childrens' GCSE coursework, but perhaps they were asked politely. I remain in my room. Oddly, Treasure remains in hers. She is silent. I call Mrs B back. An atmosphere of misery and exhaustion pervades our home. Our days are often filled with these violent mood fluctuations – paradise one minute, hell the next.

Treasure shuffles into my room later. 'Would you like to see my work?' We trudge back into her room. There, on the floor, are acres of stunning coursework. I utter suitable praise. Enfeebled by the earlier drama, it is difficult for me to be effusive. I still feel compelled to ask Treasure why, after a lifetime of shopping, she suddenly felt that the shops would close at 3.30 p.m., before I finished my phone-call?

Treasure is ever so quiet. She mumbles away with her back to me fiddling with the dread coursework. She panicked, she says. She's very sorry. Her friends' GCSE results recently came through, laden with As. Treasure looked at her work and felt a failure. Would she too get hundreds of As? Can you get Ds and still be loved?

Yes. For the next three days Treasure is a paragon. She washes up, she makes tea, she becomes a swot. But there are hundreds more days to go until Treasure's own real exam week with nine more exams. Will we make it?

Treasure's Illness

Sunday afternoon. Treasure feels sick. She does look rather pasty. She suspects that she has been poisoned by the chicken tikka sandwich she bought last night.

I am not pleased. I have always urged the Treasure to eat at home rather than squander her pocket money on salmonella sandwiches, but she would defy me and this is the result – another Sunday laid waste.

Treasure refuses all sustenance, retires to bed at 4 p.m. and stays there until Monday morning. She has spent Saturday night at Daisy's house. Whatever can they have been doing there? Was there a mother on patrol?

She awakes on Monday looking even sicker and calls weakly for a bowl. The word School debilitates her further. Is she pretending? I am often suspicious of Treasure's illnesses. They are at their worst first thing in the morning, recovery often beginning at 3 p.m. and almost completed by 6 p.m., telephone time. There is often a relapse the next morning.

Perhaps Treasure confuses exhaustion with illness.

Being woken at 7.30 a.m. after a gruelling weekend of relentless hedonism and poisoned sandwiches is not a pleasant sensation. Treasure possibly interprets it as a genuine affliction.

'I feel sick,' she moans at lunch-time. 'I'm very hungry.' She gollups down some pasta. 'I feel sicker.' She returns to bed.

'Send her to school,' shout my Advisors. 'Don't be so wet.' I should perhaps carry her lifeless form to the car, drive her to school and lay her on the cold school steps wrapped in a blanket, but I don't. Treasure remains in bed, sleeping her life away. I keep a sharp look-out for signs of recovery: a smile, a sprightly response to the telephone, dressing-up smartly in her bedroom, application of lipstick.

This time Treasure does none of it. She ignores the television, she plays no tapes. Can this be a real illness? Or is she worn to a frazzle raving, smoking and drinking? Treasure denies everything. She has done nothing untoward. She is Snow White.

'What time did you go to bed at Daisy's,' I snap.

'Early,' moans Treasure, 'but I was talking and talking to Daisy and then somebody said 'turn the light out' and then we realised it wasn't the light, it was morning.'

I ban Treasure from staying the night at Daisy's house or entertaining at our house unsupervised. I suspect Treasure and Daisy of consuming my Vodka. One inch of it remains, flavoured with water. I have no proof of course, but I haven't drunk it, Selina upstairs hasn't drunk it and the dog dislikes spirits. One whiff and its nose goes sideways.

46   Treasure is horrified by my accusation. She swears

blind that she is innocent and that Daisy is of flawless character. She staggers to an armchair next to the telephone. Injured by my cruel allegations, she needs a friend to talk to. She lifts the receiver and begins to dial, but then stops, shocked to find that she has not the strength to go on. She cannot keep her arm raised long enough to dial the whole number. She is too ill to phone. In our house we don't need a thermometer.

The Birthday

This is annual pinnacle of anxiety week in our home. It leads to Treasure's birthday. It is also mock GCSE exam week. We walk on eggshells, we breathe tension. Treasure is torn by conflicting demands. She must revise, but she must also organise three days of relentless festivities involving a cast of thousands. The number of phone-calls required is stupendous. Treasure is on all systems go in all areas: social skills, strategy, imagination, organisation *and* study.

The word 'birthday' is poison to me. It heralds wrinkles, crumbling teeth, general decay and a step nearer to the grave, but to the Treasure it is the gateway to paradise. She dreams of it throughout the year, often beginning to plan it in the Spring. This year has been comparatively laid back. Planning did not begin until August. She is desperate to be grown-up and have a fun time. She has not yet realised that these two states are more or less incompatible.

The week staggers on. Treasure revises, plans, phones,

shrieks and tries to eat and sleep. We buy The Present – another segment of hi-fi. This gives her the strength to continue. To assist Treasure in her endeavours, every item in the house is labelled in French. We talk ceaselessly of the Blitzkrieg and Liberal Reforms. Treasure darts feverishly from Hitler to hi-fi.

And before we know it, it is Thursday, exams are over, Treasure can devote herself completely to the organising: a meal out with friends on Friday, raving on Saturday, and on Sunday, the actual birthday, when only a shadow of the Treasure remains, she plans to spend an hour or two with her Mother, having tea and birthday cake.

Treasure clamps herself to the telephone to finalise plans. Things are going swimmingly – and then a catastrophe, a last minute let down which turn the plans to ashes. Delilah cannot come. She wishes to do something else. We are appalled at her treachery. A thousand more phone-calls are now essential if the arrangements are to be salvaged. Treasure cannot live one minute longer without reassurance. Will anyone else change their minds? Will they all be coming to the meal? How many more traitors are lurking about out there?

None. The terror subsides. Delilah relents, the friendship is repaired, the plans will go ahead. And they are revolutionary. This is the first time ever that Treasure has not demanded a party. She has not begged for mass ice-skating facilities, Karaoke, disco with DJ, mountains of food and going-home bags, all to be provided by an invisible mother. This time she wishes to go out. She has made her own plans. And she has rejected the usual choc cake. She wants a plain sponge decorated in pink and white covered in icing flowers. The era of Romance must be taking over. It has probably already set in.

Then suddenly, the night before the Birthday, Treasure begins to sink into a pit of gloom. 'I feel depressed,' says she looking wraithlike. 'I don't know why.'

This week has obviously taken its toll, what with the planning, revision, treachery and tension, and Treasure is already enfeebled. She is comforted by the new piece of hi-fi, twinkling and booming away in her room. Feebly she lies in bed waving the remote control, listening to some of her Mother's ancient LPs.

Will Treasure make the actual Birthday? Oddly enough we already have something to celebrate. Treasure and I have not bickered all week. Our home, despite conditions of extreme stress, has been entirely squabble free. Can this be the light at the end of the tunnel?

Luckily Treasure recovers her spirits. She needs them. The birthday weekend has no recognisable days or nights but is straight fifty-two hour thrash starting at 6 p.m. on Friday.

Off swirl Treasure and her chums, out to the dinner, carousing home at 1.30 a.m. Goodbye night's sleep for me. Much as I long to know that the Treasure is safely home, I am also keen on the odd rest at night. I hear Treasure and her friends snacking and fiddling about the house until 4 a.m., then at last, silence. They have perhaps fainted briefly from exhaustion.

Early in the morning Treasure rears up again, off to
Market with the birthday money to spend, spend, shop,

spend, eat, shriek, phone and spend until the evening, then out clubbing. The Strobe is now rather *passé* and juvenile, so she goes instead to the Twirlabout, a more thrilling venue to the east of the city. She is bringing chums home for a sleepover, so the chance of a night's sleep for me is again more or less nil. But I try. I go to bed, I put the light off, just like a normal person, and fall asleep.

Suddenly I am brutally awoken by the dog emitting its emergency alert howling bark – a hellhound baying on the landing. I also hear a strange drumming noise. We have entered the infernal regions. Quickly I fling on my dressing-gown and stagger from my room. It is 3.30 a.m. and the house is densely populated. Andrew rushes pale-faced from Treasure's bedroom. 'Don't go in there.' He bars the door. What horror can he be hiding?

'What's going on?' I am too weak to shout. Treasure appears down in the hall. She bars the door to the living room. 'Don't come in here.' I am barred from most of my house.

I can no longer tolerate the birthday activities. I ignore her request. Recklessly I enter the living room. It is clogged with youth. In the semi-darkness I see them piled about, unfamiliar figures, one large one bongoing. A particularly horrid sight at such a time.

'What the ?*?!*! is going on?' I order the visitors to leave at once. They go, ever so quietly.

'Goodbye Mum,' says the large bongo player. I must say I am surprised at their instant obedience and total lack of insolence. Treasure explains the next day. My frightful appearance terrified the life out of them: flapping gown, 51 hair on end, mascara dripping down the cheeks – a woman who has lost her grip, and so they fled in silence.

Treasure went to bed at 4 a.m. feeling rather peeved. She had been disgraced yet again by her mother, *and* on her birthday. But undefeated she is up with the lark on Sunday, still functioning and keen to go to a warehouse sale in that most charming of areas – an industrial estate close to the mouth of the Blackwall Tunnel. This is the final birthday treat, a terrifying journey after a weekend of no sleep, but we find it.

It is Treasure's dream come true – acres of super-bargain clothes and giant plastic sacks to put them in. Off she goes again – shop, spend, shop, shop. She collects a mountain of garments and so do I. The birthday improves no end. We are united by success and back in time for tea and the pink iced cake. Treasure is now fifteen and her wardrobe runneth over. It will keep her happy for a little while.

Friday Nights

Just another ordinary Friday night at our house. Treasure's friends begin to congregate on their way to a wild party. I am going out to a sedate dinner at the Gardener's house. Suddenly, from my relaxing bath, I hear the sounds of a battle. Treasure and Rosie are squabbling fiercely on the landing.

'You cow, that's a lie. She never said that.'

'Yes she did. Don't you call me a liar. I hate you.'

'You *!*!?**!'

'You're a *!**!' Slap, scratch, slap. Rip, slap, slap. A fearful sound of fisticuffs. I leap from my bath, but too late. There is Rosie rushing down the stairs shouting a crude farewell and followed by Chloe, her minder.

Treasure stamps into the bathroom flushed from battle. 'You didn't come and help. You could have stopped it, but you just said, "Where's the blue towel?" when I was calling you to help me.'

Treasure often denudes the bathroom of towels, dropping them in damp piles in distant rooms – an annoying habit, which this evening perhaps blinded me to more pressing problems.

Our evening is now in ruins. Rosie and Chloe are wandering the streets, Robert and Lizzie are late, Treasure is agitated and alone and my departure is delayed. Eventually some youths appear to escort Treasure to the party, not my favourites, but vital if the evening is to be salvaged.

Yet again my composure is done for. Can I rely on Treasure, in her present state of emotional uproar, to shut all the doors and windows? Will she leave her keys dangling in the lock (as she has already done twice this week) a boon to opportunist burglars? I plod on with my evening.

Treasure phones me later at Gardener's house. 'Good news,' says she. 'we've made up. But please can we stay longer? Please. Just half an hour?'

Yes. Then I can have a relaxing coffee and extra pudding. Another half-hour of peace for me. No such luck. Brring, brring, the hated telephone rings again. It is Treasure.

'Please can you come now? The party's ended early, they've thrown us out. We're all on the pavement. We're just outside the house.'

A brutal end to my evening. What sort of host casts children out into the street at night? I drive rather wildly across town to find Treasure, her friends and the truth. There they all are in a straggly crowd on the pavement.

'Guess what,' gabbles Treasure. 'Somebody broke a glass table and there were three hundred people and the mother went mad and Chloe's being sick. She's throwing up EVERYWHERE.'

There, across the road, is Chloe, a pasty drooping figure, supported by the Gang. We arrange her in the front seat of the car, her head hanging out of the window. Luckily the throwing up seems to have stopped. At home we lay her out in the spare room. She calls weakly for a bowl.

Leaving the the dog and Treasure in charge, I drive Rosie home. Treasure is rather browned off with this arrangement. She may have to deal with sick, but Rosie is thrilled with her evening.

As we drive we run through the list of events: a fight, a reunion, a crazed mother, a ruined home, mass expulsions, throwing-up and the nerve-wracking drive home.

'And it's only Friday,' says Rosie. 'We've still got tomorrow to go.'

What luck that the Gardener is an easy going fellow. He does not mind his guest being telephoned repeatedly and summonsed mid-dinner, although it rather disturbed our study of rose catalogues.

I must admit I am rather cheesed off with rose catalogues. Gardener has an endless supply of them and likes to gaze slowly at each variety, describing its faults and merits in depth. I have already asked for a fat, heavily scented, very dark red rose. Gardener produces a whole catalogue of fat, heavily scented dark red ones. Being so easy going, he is not aware that he is soon to be smacked over the head with a rose catalogue. My leisure opportunities are sometimes rather dismal – catalogues or sick.

Half-Term

Treasure is not one for moderation. Believing that holidays are to relax in, she relaxes ferociously for every second of half-term. And in order to relax she needs company. Perhaps the birthday weekend has given her a taste for continual revelling. A non-stop relay of chums is organised, occasionally a single one, but more often a cluster or horde.

We have a cluster round on the first holiday afternoon to eat cakes, watch telly, diddle away the evening, stay the night and stagger through some of the next morning. Treasure is able to endure a couple of hours of solitude during the afternoon, by sleeping.

She awakes refreshed and ready to go. Quickly she must be off to join another horde at another house, preferably with absent parents. She stays the night, awakens, has a quick water fight, then rushes to another rendezvous, then back, just in time for dinner and the next visiting cluster.

In they come, stoke up, then off to the Strobe. They

return. I know this because Treasure wakes me in a considerate way at 1.30 a.m.

'I'm back,' says she cheerily. 'I thought you'd like to know. I came home early.'

She is back with two chums to keep her company through the night. They awake at lunch time and pillage the larder, then off to the market, then back to refuel. I catch one of them at the fridge snatching a favourite fruit corner yoghurt. This cluster stays.

'What can we eat?' asks Treasure, staring wildly into the larder. Stocks are diminishing rapidly. They are down to cheese and biscuits and emergency tinned produce. They watch a video, probably stuffed with gratuitous sex and violence. They play guitars and sing into the night. Much as I hate to crush self-expression, I demand silence.

Half the week has gone. The word 'homework' has been mentioned fleetingly, a vague chore to be done sometime light years away in the future. I grind my teeth waiting for signs of it. Nothing happens. I am advised that this is now Treasure's responsibility, she must organise it herself, but will she? Not a chance, as far as I can see. She is exhausted from relaxing.

I ban overnight clusters for the rest of the week. Treasure takes a sack of homework to a friend's house. She cannot play or work alone. She rings merrily in the morning. In the background I hear the revelling hordes. The mother is absent, probably off slaving away to maintain another ravaged larder.

'I'm not coming home till I've finished my homework,' says Treasure dutifully.

'Won't that be difficult with all those people there?' I

suggest that she spend one evening alone in her own house. This suggestion sends the Treasure into a cold sweat. She stutters a response. When does she have to be home? She whispers, hoarse with terror.

A monstrous spectre looms before her – the Other Extreme: the end of holidays, beginning of bedtime, home-work, school and evenings at home with her mother. Treasure is terrified to death of it. Other people call it everyday life.

But if Treasure cannot have constant physical contact with her chums, she can at least have fairly constant telephone contact. Her friendship with Delilah is proving rather costly. Every event, conversation and thought must be instantly relayed. My telephone bill tells me this. It is a monstrous three hundred and nineteen pounds. The word Bristol appears in clusters, signifying a distant paramour, perhaps that pleasant hippy from last year's Glastonbury, but Delilah's number is the winner. It appears in recur-ring rashes throughout. I notice it three times in one minute.

And all this *with* Call Barring installed. But what use is a simple British Telecom device when pitted against the Treasure? She has a dozen ploys to render the barring ineffectual. Or I might forget the barring for a minute or two, then she is on it like a shark to blood. I suspect she can smell the unbarred state. And she can do ring-back – make it ring once, snatch it up, shout 'Hallo' as if a chum has rung in, then quickly dial out to nineteen others. But no longer. My fully itemised bill has revealed all. I order

Treasure to pay a large chunk of it herself.

'Delilah has Mercury. It's free after seven,' says she in a pitiful way, implying personal deprivation. Delilah drives a car, has an Apple Mac, some lovely new stripey trousers from Top Shop and a monthly allowance. Treasure has none of these things. Yet. She sits meekly by the telephone looking destitute. It is at times like this that I long for Mandatory World Socialism of the kind practised by Jesus Christ. Then Treasure and Delilah would be forced to wear simple frocks and sandals (or uniform low cost trainers) and give their luxury possessions to the less fortunate.

Luckily Delilah does not have a mobile phone. Harriet has. She is a new friend and much admired.

'Harriet has a mobile,' says Treasure, enchanted by this bit of apparatus. 'She brought it to the Strobe, then she rang David on his because it was so crowded and we couldn't be bothered to find him, and guess what? He was right next door to us in the men's lavatories.' Treasure swirls round the kitchen with a pretend mobile. 'When can we have one?'

'Never.' Foolishly I remind Treasure that Harriet called in her absence. She darts like lightening to the phone. It is unbarred. Too late I realise my mistake. She will be phoning Harriet on the mobile at 37 pence a minute. Pounds have already been babbled away. I detach her at once. Were Harriet to usurp Delilah we should be bankrupt in a flash.

Thank heavens Delilah is never likely to acquire a mobile. One thing less to covet. It's the monthly allowance that is now turning Treasure green. 'It's to pay for fares, lunches, clothes *and* pocket money,' she blabs, playing into my hands. As I pay for fares, lunches and most clothes while Treasure fritters her pocket money on luxuries, I realise that I am shelling out more than Delilah's mother. Dazzled by the huge monthly sum involved, Treasure has failed to notice this.

'Perhaps a monthly allowance is a good idea,' I say slyly. Treasure perks up enormously. What a useful thing a best friend is.

My Birthday Outing

Treasure is to take me out to dinner on my birthday. Off we go to the Rock Island Diner, my choice. As the years whiz by and I approach bus-pass time, my birthday requests become more childish. What luck that nearly half a century on, my early favourites, Elvis and Little Richard, have become rather modish.

We drive to Piccadilly Circus in the drizzling rain, both exhausted after a gruelling day at school. Treasure is thrilled by the sights and night life. So are thousands of damp tourists. Suddenly Treasure turns pale with anxiety. We have heard that in the birthday restaurant, waitresses dance on tables.

'I hope it won't be full of horrid men,' says she grimly.

'Why should it be?'

'Well, if all those waitresses are dancing on tables.' She needn't have worried. The place is packed with elderly crones like myself, having birthdays and requesting ancient tunes. The waitresses, and waiters, dance safely on the bar and no one looks at their knickers. Uninhibited customers join in. The atmosphere is rather wild, DJ sings Happy Birthday repeatedly and Treasure is dead keen to come here on *her* birthday.

She pulls out her saved up pocket money and pays the bill. Waitress' heart melts at the sight of such a charming child. She gazes soppily at both of us. She is right. Treasure is perfect. This outing is a roaring success. Right up to the drive home. And then Treasure mentions her plans for the future. A bombshell. She wishes to go to college and study fashion.

'I don't want to go to a posh university,' says she rebelliously.

If there's anything bound to throw me into a vile temper, it is the dropping of Hs on purpose and the insistence that anything above gutter level is posh. This is the first time that Treasure has openly subscribed to such a view.

'Not all universities are posh,' I snap. 'What do you mean, "posh"?'

'I can do what I like,' shouts Treasure defiantly. 'I don't want to go to university. I don't have to if I don't want to.'

'Do what you like,' I growl at Treasure. I am unable to enthuse over her choice of career in a supportive way. Every Advisor on earth has insisted that I do so, but I cannot. My secret plan is to shove Treasure to the heights of academic achievement, and so compensate for my own wasted youth. The plan is so secret that even I wasn't aware of it until this ghastly moment.

'You went to art school,' shrieks Treasure. 'Why can't I?'

62   'And it was a terrible mistake. I wish I hadn't.' I see

a tragic future for Treasure, staggering up and down Oxford Street studying *Vogue*, instead of glued studiously to Beowulf and Smollett in the Bodleian. This is a blow to me on my birthday. Treasure is obviously following in my foolish footsteps.

'I'd just like to say one thing,' she shouts. 'I am GOING to say it because YOU always say it to me.'

'Say it then.' I speak sullenly, a selfish reactionary exposed.

'I've just spent a lot of money on you, and you're STILL being horrid to me.'

The Message

I enter the house with Gardener. As yesterday was my birthday we have been on one of our dull outings to the cinema. The answerphone is flashing away. Two messages for Treasure, both unspeakably vile. Unprintable. A maniac must have left them. The same maniac twice. He has left his name shamelessly – Bill.

We are horrified. The script closely resembles a snuff movie. Can the Treasure know such a coarse person? Do I remember a Bill among her chums? Only vaguely. From what pit of depravity can such a creature have crawled? Possibly the Strobe.

'Tell the parents,' clamour my Advisors. 'Inform the police.' We remove the tape in case it may be needed for future police investigations. I collect the Treasure later and warn her, as we drive home, of the odious message that awaits her.

'Oh I heard it,' says she carelessly. 'Didn't I delete it?'

'No you did not. Who is Bill?'

'You know. He's Peter's friend.'

I express my opinion of Bill and ban him forever from our home.

'Calm down, calm down,' says Treasure, bored to death. 'It was only a joke.'

I repeat Bill's refrain, just in case Treasure hadn't heard it properly. 'How is that funny?'

'Oh that,' says she, faint with ennui. 'That's from a song.' She names the group responsible. The fiend on the telephone was merely singing a bit of modern ballad to my daughter, all about sex, death and bullets. To the Treasure this is no more distressing than a butterfly. I often wonder if there is anything on earth rude enough to give her a shock. She seems to trip through this hideous world unruffled, a flower on a dung-heap.

Tonight she is to meet the gang at Camden Town station, Mecca of the wretched. As she is not allowed to loiter in such a place alone at night, I take her in the car. While we wait the homeless slumber in piles on the pavement, the starving pick through dustbins and inebriates stagger about vomiting and shouting.

This is Treasure's playground. In it she maintains a bouyant mood. She passes it daily on the way to school and comes home with tales of her travels.

'I gave my chips to this woman. She was covered in blood, all over her face and down her coat. I'm just going to watch *Neighbours*.'

This evening the Gang is late. We sit and wait in the car. A grime-scented breeze rustles the litter, punks and yobbos hang about, civilisation decays, the country crumbles. Then the Gang pour out of the station, shrieking and laughing gaily. Off they go, out to play regardless.

65

I have taken Treasure to many such tawdry rendezvous. She finds them all delightful. As I drive home I wonder what, if anything, about the modern world might distress Treasure. Yesterday morning springs to mind. Treasure realised that our clean washing was not very fragrant. Everyone else's was. I, alone among mothers, had failed to use a scented fabric softener. Suddenly Treasure felt desolate. She had seen that life can be dismal and harsh.

Late Nights

For several weeks now Treasure has felt somewhat under the weather on Sundays. She is either comatose, or awake but vile-tempered. Could this be the result of her all-night raving, chatting, fiddling about and holding or attending sleepovers on Saturday nights? I ask. No. Treasure sees no connection. She still fights tooth and nail to stay out until 3 a.m.

And she holds a trump card. As she is forbidden absolutely to travel home alone late at night, she must wait for a friend to accompany her. Naturally no friend would dream of leaving a venue before 2.30 a.m.

'I'll have to come home by myself,' sneers the Treasure, 'and you don't want me to do that, do you?'

I order her to come home in a black cab driven by a female driver or to STAY IN.

'You are the ONLY MOTHER who does this,' screeches Treasure. 'Why are you so horrible to me? *Everyone else* comes home when they like.'

This is a phrase I have learned to distrust. '*Everyone*

else doesn't have to go to Sports Day/has a tattoo and nose ring/has boyfriends sleeping in their bedroom,' Treasure has sworn blind in the past. It means possibly two out of a class of thirty.

This time I attempt to call Treasure's bluff. 'No they don't. Daisy Harris has to be home by twelve o'clock.'

'No she doesn't.' Treasure smirks confidently. 'You ring and ask. Go on, ring.'

I ring. Mr Harris confirms my information. Daisy came home once at 2 a.m. for a special holiday treat, otherwise it's 12 o'clock and collected by Mummy or Daddy. I relay these facts to Treasure. It makes not a speck of difference.

'That is NOT TRUE,' she roars. 'He is lying.' Treasure is running her own personal corrupt police state. She disregards all evidence that displeases her. 'Anyway,' says she in a suddenly ominous tone, '*he* has no idea what Daisy does.'

'She comes home at a reasonable hour.'

Treasure assumes an expression of pity. I and the Harris parent know nothing of Daisy's and Treasure's private lives. We may think we do, but we don't. He and I are dupes together, as are many parents. We leave our homes for a weekend or an evening in a pathetic, trusting way, and no sooner are we out of sight than the word goes round: 'Free house at Treasure's/Delilah's/Andrew's/Daisy's.' Cars, taxis and buses are commandeered and London's youth floods to the adult-free zone to do God knows what.

I have gone away and returned to find the crockery crammed with dog-ends, the waste bins stuffed with beer cans. I no longer have a drinks cabinet. It has been repeatedly drained in a flash in my absence. Vodka is the favourite. Treasure is blasé about this evidence.

'It wasn't me,' she answers, bold as brass. 'I didn't drink it/smoke it/mess it up. But I'll pay for it. Take it out of my pocket money.' She is Treasure the Martyr, a popular role. She plays it now for all she is worth.

'All right,' says she, staring upwards in a saintly way. 'I'll get there at 10.30, leave at 11.30, get home at 12.30, that gives me ONE HOUR there. Oh thank you very much!' She tries again. 'Two o'clock?'

We bargain: '12.30.'/'1.30?'/'One o'clock.'/'I hate you.' We have reached a compromise, a partial victory for me.

But prospects look grim. My friend Mrs N tells me that she has recently heard of a rapist cab-driver on the go in North London and is worried to death about her daughter. 'Get a black cab,' begged Mrs N, 'not a mini-cab.'

'Yeah, yeah,' said the daughter annoyingly.

She is forty-one. It never ends.

Often, as I lay in bed worrying, sweating, unable to sleep, waiting for Treasure to come home alive, I wonder how long one can go on doing this – living in a state of near permanent fright. I am worn to a frazzle. Perhaps I need a distraction.

Gardener takes me out dancing. This makes a change. Treasure is staying in and her mother is going out raving.

'Where are you going?' asks the Treasure, interrupting her own telephone conversation to enquire. She *must* know which venue we have chosen. She is stunned by my strange behaviour. I name the club.

69

'You're joking.' Treasure snorts into the phone. 'My Mum's going to Paradise with her *boyfriend*.' She laughs in a mocking way. 'Let's go and watch them.'

We leave Treasure sneering happily on the telephone. While I am out she may glue herself to it for hours on end. With any luck she will be unable to wrench herself away from it and spy on my dancing.

No wonder she fancied a look. Gardener and I are rather out of place at this venue. No one else is over eighteen. But where are the elderly meant to go for a dance? Occasionally, when Gardener is not droning softly about plants, he likes to go wild, as he did in his youth. He is rather less inhibited while dancing than I am. But it is *my* child who may be lurking and sneering with her chums at the edge of the dance floor. And this outing was meant to be anxiety-free.

Waking Up

Treasure has enormous difficulty waking up in the mornings. She has had this difficulty for the last ten years.

'I can't move,' she cries weakly. 'I don't feel well. Look, I'm shaking.' With a huge effort she lifts one arm, but her strength soon fails. The arm flops back, the eyes close, Treasure moans in a heartrending way. 'Just leave me alone,' she begs. 'I must have more sleep. Just ten minutes.'

I persevere. I have tried everything: a pleasant greeting, orange juice, curtains wrenched open, Big Breakfast on, dog wandering in to give her a kiss, louder and harsher orders to get up, removal of bedclothes and even the cold flannel in the face. Treasure only changes from limp to fiercely defiant.

'I'm ill,' she shouts. 'Can't you see? I CANNOT GET UP.'

Nor can she eat a speck of breakfast. 'Take it away,' moans Treasure, recoiling and gagging feebly at the sight of it.

Eventually she rises and lurches, pallid and glumpy,

'I'm meant to be like this,' she announces,
vindicated by television research, 'It's normal, I'm not lazy.'

about the room. But this is only a tiny step on the road to normal function. She must now find her clothes, a major stumbling block.

'Why didn't you get them ready last night?'

'I was asleep last night. I WAS TIRED.' Despite ten years of bitter experience she has still not quite grasped the purpose of preparing things in advance.

Today she cannot find suitable tights. She rarely can. They are all laddered. Once upon the Treasure's body a pair of tights is in immediate danger. Were they 700 denier chain-mail they would still be laddered in a trice. Reduced to penury by the repeated purchase of tights, I have taken to mending them. Treasure loathes mended tights. They are not chic. Her fury intensifies. Then her skirt disappears. The skirt and I have conspired to delay her.

'Where is it?' she scrabbles hopelessly at the dense carpet of mangled clothing. 'You MADE me take it off when you took my shirt.' What can she mean? As Treasure shrieks and searches, time whizzes by. Late again. She leaves in a bate. She is weak with hunger, has lost her hairband and is late for French. Repelled by life, she stamps sluggishly off up the road.

'Leave her alone,' say my Advisors, shocked by this carry-on. 'Let her be late.'

I leave her alone. She is late again and again. Later and later. Once I have left the house for work she will sink back into a coma until lunch-time, wake up briefly for *Neighbours*, doze until tea-time, and then wake properly, refreshed by her lovely sleep, full of energy, alert and dynamic. Naturally she then cannot sleep at bed-time.

Soon she becomes nocturnal, her body clock stymied. I would like to give my Advisors a sharp slap.

We are pelted with useless advice from all sides. The television has been at it too. It recently informed Treasure that the teenage body functions better late at night and that stupor and inertia in the mornings is a normal condition for a creature of her age.

'I'm meant to be like this,' she announces triumphant, vindicated at last. 'It's normal. I'm not lazy.' Her bedtime, blessed by television researchers, is now officially 4 a.m.

I remember seeing a charming and stunningly effective New York headmaster on television a year or so ago. He would patrol the corridors of his Bronx school with a megaphone and baseball bat and huge teenagers would spring to attention and function efficiently, even first thing in the morning. Perhaps he could come and stay in our house. This is our only hope.

But it's no good dreaming of Bronx headmasters. I must do as the Advisors tell me and be firmer and more consistent. Treasure must go to bed earlier. I will no longer allow her to stay out all night during term-time. No more staying at friends' houses. Even on Saturdays.

I feel impelled to enforce this rule to save Treasure from wrecking her life. Freedom to stay out has led to twenty-five late slips, six Mondays in a coma, ten wasted Sundays, three detentions, two suspensions and a further deterioration of manners.

Exhausted and debilitated by her life of pleasure, the Treasure has not a speck of energy left for her studies. I receive yet another drubbing from Headmistress.

74   'Treasure's lifestyle is not compatible with academic

success,' says she strictly. She is obviously losing patience with my weediness.

I insist that Treasure stay in.

'You can't keep me prisoner in this house,' she screams. 'You can't.' But I must. If Treasure is to go down the tube, then I feel she must wait at least until after GCSEs.

But Treasure is not alone in her prison. Relays of visitors turn up. 'Delilah's come round to do her homework with me,' says she studiously. 'Isn't that nice of her?' Both retire to Treasure's room. Loud chatter, bongoing and the stench of jossticks pour from it.

I shout from the stairs. 'That doesn't sound like homework,' but Treasure cannot hear me. She is protected by a wall of sound. I enter her room.

'Get out,' shrieks Treasure rudely. 'How dare you come in my room without saying?' Unknown to her I have been screaming myself hoarse outside her chamber for several minutes prior to entering.

'Don't dare tell me to get out. Get on with your homework or Delilah can go home. And tidy this up.'

Treasure's room is purgatory. It is solid with mess, noise and sickly aromas. The normal person, entering this den, would sink into a dead faint. It is in this atmosphere that Treasure affects to study.

Treasure changes tactics from abusive to martyr. She clamps her little mouth shut, goes pale and murmurs in a voice of pain. 'Will you please leave us alone.'

Sometimes, through the fog of misunderstanding, Treasure can detect that her mother is approaching blast-off. Silence falls upon her room. Treasure and Delilah work without a sound for twenty minutes. Or perhaps snooze, or whisper. How can I tell? And this silence can never endure while we have a telephone.

Knowing that Treasure has been incarcerated by her cruel mother, supportive chums are ringing in their hundreds to keep her in touch with the outside world. Scarcely has she settled down to her studies than 'Brrring, brrring,' a disturbance.

I order them to ring back later, but the damage is done. Treasure can no longer concentrate. She knows she is missing something. What can it be? Her thoughts wander about, guessing, pondering: Who's broken up with who? Who's pulled who? Who's got her ribbed, black jumper? Will she have it back by Saturday night?

What hope for Macbeth? How can he get a toe in there? Does Headmistress know what she is asking of me?

Fame

Treasure comes home enraptured from the Twirlabout Club. 'We've been talent-spotted,' she sings, whizzing about the living-room. 'We're going on Late Night Blah. This woman came over and invited us. Me and Delilah, because we're so good at dancing and we can take seven friends.'

Naturally the phone is in constant use for days – people calling in and arranging, screeching, cancelling and rearranging. The whole world is clamouring for an invite. No one has a hope in hell of getting through to me. Gardener tries and fails. Should any of my friends hit a chink in phone usage, Treasure answers briskly and insolently. Her priorities lie elsewhere – organising, selecting and inviting.

Gardener arrives late for dinner and in a fury. His attempts to reach me by telephone were met with such stunning rudeness by the Treasure that he feels impelled to reprimand her. He goes upstairs to do so. From the kitchen I hear a strange and terrible roaring sound. It is

Gardener screaming. He returns to the kitchen flushed and shaking.

I have never seen him in a fury. He has never been in one, not since his divorce ten years ago. Terrible things have happened to him through those ten years: a mad gunman took over his flat, someone stole all his photographic equipment, more burglars banged a hole in his ceiling, all his savings were stolen, then his car. But he never lost his temper. Until now. In some areas Treasure is uniquely skilled.

This must be a thrilling TV programme to cause such uproar. I have never seen it. Neither has Grandma. It is way past our bedtimes. Rashly Grandma tells her respectable elderly friends in Hove of the Grandchild's debut upon the screen.

The big day arrives. More and more chums pack themselves into the Treasure's room to try on outfits, scream, change, swap outfits, scream, apply make-up and perfumes and scream. Now and again the door opens and an exotically dressed girl bursts out on a blast of hot perfume. At last they all emerge, looking outrageous and rather *risqué*. This is a deliberate ploy to attract the cameras.

I am now quite keen for them to leave. At last they are off. The house is silent and we are able to relax. Bliss. Valiantly we try and remain awake to watch our own Treasure on the telly, video tape in position. Down in Hove Grandma is poised in bed with her lemon tea and hot water bottle, remote control in hand.

On goes the programme. Horrors. It features sex, loud music, violence, simulated sex, horror films, jokes about sex, rather a lot of sweating and writhing, ripped clothing, bare bosoms and more sex, with our own Treasure and

78

her chums dancing about in a rather brazen way between features.

Several lady pensioners in Hove have probably fainted. I gawp at this depravity for fifteen minutes and go to bed in despair. What has the world come to? With what vile thoughts is the Treasure's mind now irredeemably sullied? But I am soon awakened by the telephone. It is Grandma, appalled by what she has seen.

'What a load of **!*!' she roars. 'And I told all my friends to watch it,' She is deeply ashamed. 'What's she doing on a bloody disgusting programme like that? She's no right to be there.' Try as she might Grandma cannot refrain from criticism. 'Why did you allow it?' she bellows. 'You should never have let her go.'

This is rather unjust. I expected something in the style of Top of the Pops, some vile music, some perhaps mildly erotic dancing, but not this iniquitous stew, this taste of a brutish demi-monde, by which the Treasure and her chums will now be forever tainted.

At last Grandma rings off, weakened by shock and regret. Will she now be shunned by her more respectable friends? I fall asleep again, only to be wakened at 2 a.m. by a chorus of hellish screams. What can it be? Waves of screams rise repeatedly from the living room. I totter downstairs for a look. It is Treasure and friends in a row on the sofa, bright and rosy-cheeked with happiness and excitement, watching themselves on the video. Every appearance initiates mass screaming.

Screaming seems to have been this week's main feature. For some of us it has not been pleasant.

After years of gargantuan telephone bills and now goaded on by Gardener's bitter experiences while trying to get through to me, I have decided to purchase a payphone. I have threatened and warned Treasure for months of my intentions. Bill after bill has passed, each more huge than the last, as the Treasure has failed time after time to control her telephoning. Day after day, enraged chums, relatives, employers and possibly admirers, have tried and failed to contact me. Our phone is engaged forever.

Now and again, when the Treasure is out, or perhaps asleep or busy with chums and the coast is clear, I have tip-toed to the phone and quickly dialled a friend, or the friend may have cleverly managed to reach me, but suddenly Treasure appears on the spot, as of magic. A seventh sense has told her that someone else is using the telephone. She realises at once that she must use it that minute. There she is, by my side, begging and screaming for me to stop talking and hand the precious instrument over to her.

My chat is sabotaged. I can no longer hear it. Treasure becomes more desperate by the second, dishevelled and weeping, her phone-call a matter of life or death.

I have now had enough of all this and have hardened my heart. My phone is to be barred at all times and the Treasure will have a payphone upstairs and weekly allowance to use on it.

She has not accepted this information. The payphone still comes as a ghastly shock to her. She returns from school one ordinary day and there is the horrid thing installed in her room.

80   'I am NOT having that phone,' she roars. 'How *could* you

do that without asking me? It is the WRONG SORT.' She would have preferred the BT squillion pound variety. 'I am not using it. TAKE IT BACK.'

But she is forced to try it. It gobbles up ten pences and allows Treasure only a few seconds of speech.

'It doesn't work,' screeches Treasure in a frenzy. 'It only lasts two seconds. Now you've GOT to change it.'

'It only needs adjusting.' I remain calm. I know that in only a few hours Gardener will arrive, read the instruction book in an unruffled way, adjust the phone and we shall be saved. I have tried myself, but am unable to comprehend the instructions with Treasure bellowing and glaring.

Meanwhile, even before Gardener arrives, our life improves. As Treasure's friends ring through in their hundreds I am now able to briskly instruct them to ring her upstairs on another number. Then Treasure may dash to her very own phone and chatter endlessly, undisturbed and hidden away from her mother. She is in paradise up there, rushing to answer her own phone again and again.

The only snag is Gardener's rather sullen behaviour when asked to do the telephone adjustments.

'Why can't you do it?' he asks bossily. 'It's quite straight-forward.'

It is not. It is incomprehensible, but to Gardener, an instruction manual, like a catalogue, is a gripping read. He often sits about bolt upright for days on end mulling over manual after manual, and then, for a treat, he will jump up and mend a complex bit of equipment – a teasmade, a toaster, a car. I assumed that he would

81

be in heaven playing with our payphone, but no. He is rather morose and sulky.

I have a dream – that one day everyone will behave themselves properly all the time. So far, only the dog can do this.

Festive Season

I am lying in what I hoped would be a pleasant and relaxing bath, when suddenly I realise that Christmas is only a few weeks away. What a drear prospect. I immediately start to weep. This is a poignant time of year, when people without families think they are missing something pleasant, and people with families squabble and sulk and torment each other. We are in the second grouping.

Last year we had a nerve-racking Christmas. Treasure and Grandma clashed on Christmas morning, jeopardising our lunch and whole holiday period.

As I opened my present from the Treasure, some delightful crystal goblets which have emptied her bank account, I noticed that one was already broken. Treasure was devastated.

'Why did you buy something so expensive that you knew would break?' roared Grandma, the Queen of Tact. Treasure ran sobbing from the room, her Christmas in ruins. Her language as she left was a dreadful fright. It ruined Grandma's Christmas.

Does Christ know, I wonder,
what his birthday can do?

'This is my last Christmas,' shouted Grandma pessimistically, 'and *she's* spoilt it. And I shall tell her so. I'll come back next year and *haunt* her.' This was perhaps staggeringly harsh, but people do tend to go wild at Christmas. Grandma wept in the kitchen. Treasure wept up in her bedroom. The turkey cooked in the oven. It was Jesus' birthday and our house was in uproar. And we are not even Christian. Would we make it as far as lunch?

'I'm not sitting at the table with her,' shouted Grandma.

Upstairs Treasure continued to weep passionately. 'Why do you always stick up for *her*?' I do not. I tried to reassure the Treasure. Downstairs I had been fighting her corner, but she was inconsolable.

Luckily we were invited to Christmas drinks with the Perez family next door. Treasure remained in her room paralysed with misery. Grandma stamped round to the Perez' and described our hideous morning. There was Mrs P's daughter, sitting on the sofa amidst her family being delightful. Mrs P pointed this out to Grandma.

'Look at her now,' said Mrs P, gazing lovingly at her charming daughter. Naturally Grandma and I were envious. Would this ever happen to us? I remembered the Perez girl in her youth sitting on windowsills dangling her legs provocatively and whistling at passing boys, while behind her the house shook with thunderous pop music, enraging the neighbours. But there she was, turned into a perfect girl.

Meanwhile, I knew that the Treasure still lay sobbing in her bedroom missing the festivities. Does Christ know, I wonder, what his birthday can do?

Will this year be any better? We plunge into the   85

preparations pretending that it will. Treasure is keen to have a giant tree. She always is. Last year's was bent at the top, its fairy squashed sideways by the ceiling. The tree must be drowning in cascades of decoration and glitter. For some silly reason I am also keen on a tree – the smell of pine, the twinkling lights, the surprise parcels.

Grandma is appalled by our expenditure. 'You've spoilt her,' she has shouted ferociously over the years as each new trinket appeared – the Gameboy, the bicycle, the stereo, the CDs. 'You've made a rod for your own back.' She does not understand that these items are considered essential basic requirements by the average Nineties First World child. It now costs half the Royal Mint to fill an Xmas stocking. Grandma has difficulty keeping pace with things. As a child she had an orange and a rag dolly for Christmas.

Treacherously Mrs Perez is running away to Cornwall with her children to hide. I give her a strict telling off but with no success. We shall just have to plod through it without her. But the greengrocer round the corner has a charming new line in bargain glass bobbles. I buy a dozen.

'Buy more,' commands the Treasure excitedly. 'What others has he got?'

'Bloody waste of money,' shouts Grandma.

Here we go again.

We see very little of the Treasure over these holidays. She is forever partying. This is difficult for Grandma. Now that she is spending more and more time in our house she can observe the Treasure's behaviour at first hand. It is rather more shocking than my edited version, which she has become accustomed to down in Hove, sixty miles away from the truth. How will she cope with permanent residence here? Anxiety, roaring arguments and screeching are not recommended for someone of eighty-nine with a heart condition.

I drive Grandma and the dog back to Hove, leaving Treasure alone and unsupervised in our home, always a nerve racking and risky move, *and* in the festive season, when partying, raving and drunkenness are mandatory. Will Treasure feel obliged to throw a party in our absence?

Meanwhile, Grandma is thrilled to be home again. A week or two in our house always makes her long for the solitude of her own flat. She would like the dog and I to stay with her for a holiday.

'Why don't you stay here for a few days and have a rest?' she roars. But how can I? Back in town my own home is probably a nightclub, washing-up and debris mounting up, larder emptying, windows and doors flapping open and robbers pouring in. I cannot relax in Hove and must leave Grandma alone to fight her angina.

At least she will be rid of the dog. She is rather sick of it dribbling on her carpet and furnishings and begging and barking constantly for snacks. I find these qualities endearing but Grandma does not. She too had a Boxer dog in her youth which she often allowed to sit at table on a cushioned bench. She has conveniently forgotten this fact.

The Fire

Treasure's bongoes have saved our lives. She was in her room banging away on them with two chums at 12.45 a.m. while down in the living-room Gardener and I were watching the television.

We hear a small crash from my bedroom. It must be Treasure blundering about in there borrowing tapes or lipstick or the last remaining hairbrush. Shortly there is an enormous crash. But before I have a chance to investigate, the phone rings. It is our tormented neighbour.

'Not only is your daughter playing the bongoes at 1 a.m.,' says he, 'but she also seems to be smashing up your furniture. Please make her BE QUIET.'

I rush upstairs to reprimand the Treasure, only to find black smoke billowing from my bedroom. In the next room Treasure and her chums are still bongoing away. They had thought her new Passion jossticks smelt rather unpleasant and wondered why I was smashing up furniture, but otherwise were unaware of the raging inferno next door.

The fire brigade was summoned, the blaze extinguished and my bedroom turned into a black hole. What luck that Grandma is no longer present. All bedrooms except for Treasure's are ruined by smoke – an upsetting experience for me, but Treasure seems to have escaped trauma. She is captivated by the droves of handsome firemen and begs them to save her Christmas bongoes. And she is thrilled to bits that it was my fault, not hers.

'Imagine if *I'd* left a candle on in *my* room,' she gloats. 'You'd have gone on and on. I'm going to tell Grandma.'

Treasure forgets her threat. She spends a jolly night out at her chum's house while I sleep in the stinking spare room weeping over what remains of my possessions.

But another treat lies in store for Treasure. She has left her mouldy old trainers in my bedroom. They are no more. The insurance company will now buy her another pair. This is a priority purchase. The trainers must be bought at once, before my bed, typewriter, clothing and reading glasses.

'I've got to have them today,' shrieks Treasure in a passion. 'I need them tonight.' She is going to an all-night New Year's rave and the only shoes she can possibly dance in are the unbought trainers.

Off we go to Oxford Street. Mammoth sales are being held in two gargantuan trainer shops. A drillion bargain trainers are packed onto all shelves from floor to ceiling. Treasure cleverly picks her way through them all and with a seventh sense detects a pair of non-sale super-trend trainers on display in a tiny glass-covered hole in the floor. Through the million stamping bargain-hunters' feet she has managed to spot them.

89

'I want those,' she snaps decisively. 'They're the ones Rosie nearly got.' She is blind to the treasure trove of bargains. She has hoved in on the top-price, ultrahip, rip-off-of-the-century pair and must have them. Fifty pounds for a pair of plimsolls with a star on.

Still traumatised by the fire, I buy them, and a bargain pair for me, as all my footwear has been burnt to a crisp, while all around us pallid, tight-lipped mothers are buying trainers for their treasures. I am keen for the inventor of the trainer to be shot at dawn, or released defenceless into a trainer shop such as this when I am present.

Perhaps the fire has soured my outlook on life. It has sweetened Treasure's. She is in a sunny mood as we return to the charnel-house. After all, the telephone is still working. She may tell the world about her new trainers, and better still, she has lost her old dressing gown, jeans, ear-rings and two CDs.

'They were definitely in your room,' says she. 'I saw them there.'

Following the fire, Gardener enjoys a sudden burst of popularity. He is Treasure's favourite person of the moment. Compared to her mother, he is a hero.

'Gardener saved my life.' She stares at me with tremendous scorn. '*You* didn't. You just ran downstairs and left me. I could have died in the fire.'

This is not quite accurate, but has enough of a grain of truth in it to make me feel guilty for the rest of my life. Gardener did all the right things and I didn't. It was he who sensibly closed all the doors, ordered the Treasure and her chums downstairs and saved them from the flames, while I merely ran screeching for a telephone because ours had burnt. Naturally Treasure accuses me of forgetting to save her. It is difficult for her to like Gardener and me both at once.

Piercing

One of the terrible after-effects of our fire is the end-less shopping that must follow. We now need to trudge round Camden Market looking for replacement cushions and bedspreads, spending hundreds of pounds that the insurance company has not yet coughed up.

This is hell for me and heaven for Treasure. She views the seething crowds with delight. She would live in this market if she could. It is jam-packed with tourists, hip-pies, crusties and youth buying ethnic trinkets, T-shirts, falafels, bongoes, ear-rings and candles, dithering and blocking all paths. I am keen to scream loudly, knock everybody over and run home, but I cannot. We must shop. Our house is bare and crying out for soft furnishings.

Suddenly, out of the crowds, a grubby and mutilated youth looms up ahead. His cheeks, nose, eyebrows and lips are pierced by lumps of decorative metal. I experience a horrid tingling sensation from the waist downwards and want to faint.

92 'Erk,' I groan as the nightmare vision passes.

'I can't believe how rude you are,'
Treasure snaps at me. 'He looks REALLY NICE.'

'Will you stop that,' hisses Treasure. 'You are SO RUDE.'

'It makes me feel sick,' I explain, reeling slightly, 'And anyway, he *wants* to give people a shock.'

'No he doesn't.' Treasure leaps to the horror's defence. 'He wants to look SMART.' She is terrified that her insensitive mother may have offended the fashion monster. In her eyes he is adorned in a charming way. She doesn't see the risks as I do. What if one of the metal bobbles or loops were to catch on a twig? Or a passing scarf or finger? What if someone spiteful gave the piercings a tweak? Goodbye half a cheek or nostril. Imagining ripped flesh I cling weakly to a lamp-post, buffeted by milling crowds, dreading another batch of wandering mutilations.

'Will you stop that,' snaps Treasure. 'I can't believe how rude you are. He looked REALLY NICE.' Ruthlessly she propels me into the cushion shop to think of other things.

But we cannot escape the hated piercings for long. Mrs Perez' daughter next door has recently taken to wearing an ear-ring at the very top of her ear – the bit that goes red. The ear-ring has made it go redder. Mrs Perez and I wince at the sight. We can scarcely bear to look.

What if Treasure does it? I shall be in a fairly permanent state of nausea and vapours. Treasure often threatens to pierce bits of herself, starting with nose and navel. Mrs Perez herself remains calm and recommends paradoxical injunction again. The next time Treasure mentions plans to stab lumps of metal into herself, I must affect not to mind at all.

For once I am in luck. Treasure announces her arrangements for self-mutilation at dinner when visitors are present and I have just swallowed two glasses of wine.

'I'm going to the London Piercing Centre,' says she gloating. 'Andrew's taking me.' With a thrill of anticipation, she awaits the usual uproar.

'Lovely.' The drink speaks for me. 'Isn't that nice of Andrew?'

Treasure gapes across the table. For a few rare seconds her jaw is open but motionless. 'Don't you mind?'

'No. As long as it's not somewhere cheap. As long as you get your own needle.'

Treasure returns to her room silenced. Her plan is foiled, but for how long?

'Well done,' says Gardener. 'I think it worked.' It is helpful to have a supporter. And Gardener has another attractive quality – he very rarely criticises. The only other creature with similar qualities is the dog. They are both becoming indispensible. Perhaps I should consider marriage. How odd that the minute I begin to contemplate matrimony, Treasure's opposition to Gardener increases.

'Why does *he* have to come here *every* day,' she shrieks next morning. 'He's *always* here. You never spend any time with *me*.' Although Gardener saved her life only days ago, she no longer admires him. It is difficult to know how to proceed.

The New Computer

We don't have carpet any more in our house, we have homework overlay. As Treasure grows, so does her homework. It now covers the bedroom and living-room floors.

The overlay is fairly permanent. Once spread out, its size gives Treasure a bit of a fright. How will she ever complete a task of such magnitude? She is temporarily paralysed into inactivity. She cannot do it, she cannot tidy it away. She has to accustom herself to it. It becomes a fixture. Gradually, as the days pass, the acre of homework becomes familiar. It no longer terrifies Treasure. She does a bit, she does a little more. The weeks pass. She finishes it.

Then it looks rather formidable – a carpet of achievement. Treasure rings Chloe, who has been wrestling with similar homework.

'Spread it out,' she shouts excitedly. 'If you spread it out it looks really good. I've done pages and pages.' It stays out for a day or two to be admired, and then it goes back to school, only to be replaced by the next lot.

This makes life hell for me and the dog. We cannot reach our armchairs, I cannot cross the room in a relaxed way to adjust the TV or video. The remote control is lost, buried years ago under another homework mountain. Treasure guards her homework like a lioness. We dare not tread on it or disturb it, but she cannot be criticised. She is, after all, working. She is in a state of grace.

I remember in my youth having natty little things called '*exercise books*.' They were made up of sheets of lined or plain paper, bound together in book form and unspreadable. You couldn't lose bits or muddle them up. But for some reason schools now favour the '*folder and sheets*' – perfect for scattering, muddling, mislaying and crumpling. I expect it goes with the new technology, which Treasure must also learn to cope with. She is nagging away for a computer.

'Everyone's got one except us,' moans Treasure the consumer queen, a child of the nineties unfortunately burdened with a mother still stuck in the Baroque rut.

I dread the computer – a magic porridge pot of sheets, but there is no escape. Apparently Treasure must be computer literate. And I have all the lovely insurance money from our fire. Why replace boring old furniture and carpets, when one can have a computer? I have already frittered loads of it on an ancient cello which I often sit plucking and sawing at in a primitive way. Naturally Treasure is slightly peeved. If I may wallow in the past, then she may leap into the future. She is dead keen for us to squander the remaining money on an up-to-the-minute model which can store a hundred books, write music, create art and display her work in stylish print, all at top speed.

Rashly I agree to purchase one. I too have my dreams. Fascinated by the marvels of the computer, Treasure will sit before it working away, linking up with her friend Henry, school computer genius, creating gem-like chunks of homework and forgetting all about the Strobe, Twirlabout, drugs, sex, raves, telephoning, new clothes and Sun-In. Our home will become an oasis of calm and industry.

Treasure and I can both sit on orange boxes on the bare boards playing with our new toys. The accoustics will be excellent and we never saw the carpet anyway.

The new computer has arrived. It is a monster. It can do almost anything on earth. Treasure, Henry (school computer genius and advisor) and Andrew cluster in front of it, mesmerised by its glowing screen and little boxes of instructions. They cannot tear themselves away, even for pudding.

They eat pudding around it, pecking at it in turn and fiddling with its mouse and windows. I eat my pudding alone at table.

'Mum,' roars Treasure from the Techno room, 'come and look at this. You've got to look.' She sounds tremendously excited. I run upstairs.

'Look, look.' Treasure points ecstatically at the screen. The words 'Eeeasy Treasure' wobble across it in vaguely Italic script. 'And look, look,' she shrieks. 'Eeeasy Delilah' follows. I am bitterly disappointed.

'What's that for?'

Treasure and her chums gaze at me in surprise. 'It just *does* it,' says she.

I cannot think why. For years I have fought against the coming of the computer. Now, laden with insurance money from the fire, I have given in. Personally I would go for the fountain pen with a lever, *no cartridges* and a fat nib, and when under extreme pressure, a typewriter, but Treasure is a modern child. She must learn to deal with new technology, so I am told, and anyway, she likes to lie motionless and press buttons while all around her machines click and whirr into action.

She is not the only one. Mrs H's daughter is also thrilled to pieces with the school computer club. She often stays there late after school.

'It's a strange world in there,' says Mrs H, as if returning from an alien planet. Soft but cultured music plays constantly and Teacher is a groovy guy with a pony-tail. In front of the magic screens, numerous little girls sit doing useless things.

'Look,' says the Daughter. 'I can get Marilyn Monroe up and turn her round.'

'Why?' asks Mrs H.

The Daughter ignores her and carries on excitedly. 'Interested in Art?' she asks perkily. 'Look. Here's the Mona Lisa.' Up it comes.

What for? Why not open a book instead? Mrs H and I are baffled. Meanwhile, we have to enter the modern world and learn to use the wretched things. Henry has promised to give the Treasure lessons. He promised and promised. Now, having spent most of the year diddling with computers, he is months behind with his homework

99

and forbidden to go out. Our house is filled with terrifying machinery and Henry can no longer help us.

I ask the Gardener for assistance. For days he wanders the maze of instructions, occasionally ringing Henry for advice. Eventually, eyes weakened and head throbbing, he learns to use the computer. He can now show Treasure how to do it, but she is in a sulk. She will only glower at me, the floor or at Gardener's back, as if keen to stab him. She stamps to her room mumbling. What ever for? By tea-time she can no longer contain her fury. She accosts me on the stairs.

'How dare you let *him* phone *my* friend. Will you and *your friend* please leave Henry alone. You're doing his head in. That's why he won't help me.'

Treasure has reached an impasse. She cannot use the computer alone because the instructions and booklets are incomprehensible, Gardener is not allowed to instruct her because he's my friend, I can't because I'm her mother, and Henry can't. Because.

The computer sits idly in the spare room using up space. It can't do anything.

Holiday Plans

Spring is on the way and we are in a quandary over our holiday plans. Treasure and I alone on holiday together would not be tranquil. Anyway, Treasure does not seek tranquility. She wants fairly non-stop raving, bevvies of boys and a dash of afternoon grilling on a golden beach – everything she wanted last year, but more of it and a snazzier version.

What she really longs for is a holiday without her mother. Her chums will be off to Ibiza with no mothers at all, free to go clubbing, get food poisoning and first degree sunburn, and have their fizzy drinks spiked by unscrupulous men in Antonio Town, magnet to lager louts. Treasure is desperate to join them, but the chums are older than Treasure. They are seventeen, she is fifteen and still in need of a chaperone.

I suggest a holiday with some friends of mine in Spain, where Treasure may bring a chum. This will not do. She hurls the cruel truth at her mother.

'No one will come,' she roars in despair. 'I've begged

all my friends, but no one wants to stay with YOU for a fortnight. You are the strictest most horrible mother. You're always SHOUTING.'

It has perhaps slipped her memory that throughout our last holiday in Cornwall with four of her chums I spoke in soft and measured tones at all times despite intense provocation. 'It's Spain or nothing,' say I, hard-hearted to the end.

Treasure flings herself on the telephone and continues her search for a loyal friend to suffer the holiday with her. What good are the beaches, pools and discos of the Mediterranean when a loathsome mother is present? She begs every known acquaintance to come and endure this fortnight of hell with her.

Eventually she finds some volunteers. She enters my room looking stern. 'Delilah will come,' says Treasure strictly. 'These are our conditions. We may go to discos, we may sleep as late as we want, we may go out alone in the day, we may get drunk.'

I am keen on the sleeping late. This means silent and relaxing mornings for me. The rest I will discuss with Delilah's parents.

'Can I have two friends?' asks Treasure, dredging up a tiny speck of enthusiasm. 'Lizzie says she'll come too.' I am impressed that two friends are prepared to share Treasure's suffering. 'Will there be bar football?' she asks. And will there be golden sand, water sports, giant banana and swimming pool adorned with sun-tanned boys? Without these divertissements, Treasure will not contemplate the holiday.

Not that I want her to be a sycophantic creep, but a

smidgin of gratitude would not be out of place here. Perhaps instead of an exotic sea-side holiday, a week's forced march across the Gobi desert or tour of the Brazilian slums would be more fruitful. Then upon our return, Gospel Oak Lido would seem like paradise.

I discuss the ghastly holiday predicament with Mrs Perez. She reminds me that this is the hell year for holidays. Treasure is too young to go alone and too old to go with Mummy. Her treasures also slumped about complaining at this age. Next year will be better, says she. Treasure can go with her chums and I can stay at home in the garden with the dog and watch the tadpoles in complete silence.

Mrs Perez let hers go alone when they were sixteen. They fell off motor bikes, broke their fingers, hitch-hiked, had all their money and possessions stolen, ended up in a Spanish gaol overnight and were flown home in disgrace, at vast expense to Mr and Mrs Perez. Only a couple of years to go and Treasure can fall off motor bikes and go to prison. She cannot wait.

Shopping

Treasure needs summer shoes. It is only early spring but she needs them at once, this morning in the pelting rain. We must go traipsing round the shops. This could be a pleasant outing for Treasure, but she has to take her Mother for funding, which casts a pall over things.

She heads straight for the ten-ton clogs with three-inch heels, reminiscent of the surgical boot. This does not strike me as best choice for a summer sandal. I had imagined Treasure running blithely over the Heath or skipping along beaches in light summer footwear.

Unwisely I criticise her choice. 'Aren't the heels rather high? Will they be comfortable?'

Treasure sweeps from the shop in a fury. 'I can't go on with this,' she declares dramatically. 'We're going back to the car.'

I am rather disappointed. I have just spent ages searching for a parking space, pumped a rajah's ransom into the meter and now wish to plod on with this gruelling expedition. I remain calm.

'What is your problem?' I use Treasure's vocabulary to aid communication.

'I am choosing these shoes.' Treasure grits her teeth. 'I say how much or yes or no.'

She issues further instructions: I must sit in silence on a distant seat and at a given signal scuttle up to the till with my cheque book. Should the sales assistant approach me, I must point silently at the Treasure and gaze blankly out of the window. It is still pouring down. We have lost all our umbrellas. I am keen to purchase the summer shoes so that this hideous ordeal need not be repeated for at least twelve months.

Treasure sweeps in and out of a dozen shops followed by the Silent Walking Wallet. At last she spots a suitable pair of sandals. They are lightweight and reasonably priced and the heels are a modest one-and-a-half inches. I hold my breath. Will she choose them? Or will it be the ten-ton stilts again? Then more shocks. Treasure asks my opinion. She purchases the sandals with my approval. She still likes them when she gets home, her friends are envious. Our outing seems to have been a success.

Foolishly I have rejoiced too soon. Treasure and I return to the market weeks later to purchase espadrilles for our holiday. To my mind these are flat things with rope soles that cost three pounds. But the Treasure has misunderstood. She thought the espadrille was a fashion item with elegant three inch stack heels, delicate strip of coloured canvas attaching it to the foot, ribbons tied up the ankle in a snazzy way and costing an arm and a leg. She is mortified to be offered cheap flat things. She has now set her heart on the

Boiling, exhausted and deafened
I sink to the floor. Treasure is horrified.

stilt espadrilles, besides which her new sandals are but dross.

'Erk,' says Treasure, backing away as I buy my new cheap footwear. 'They're disgusting.' Worse still, *I* have bought something and *she* hasn't. This therefore does not count as a shopping expedition. Nor does the last one, now that the sandals have been rejected. Treasure's quest for sandals continues. She vows to exchange the last pair, she will get a credit note, she will bludgeon the salespersons, she will NOT, NOT wear those sandals. She will die first.

We are still stuck at first base.

But there will be more shopping expeditions, endless days of them, because we need the rest of our holiday wardrobe. Treasure will be on the look-out for any shopping opportunity. If she spots me having a tiny read or a tea-break she will beg for a lift to Oxford Street.

'Why not? You're not doing anything.' She cannot understand my reluctance. She herself has practised regularly and is now a highly skilled shopper. She would shop for hours, even days without food or rest, travelling, searching and frittering, if only funds were available. She has even offered to shop for me.

'Give me a hundred pounds and I'll go to Sainsbury's,' says she generously, but I meanly will not trust her with the cash. And now the weeks fly by, our holiday looms and we need clothes from Top Shop. We must both go.

If there is a hell on earth for me it is Top Shop. It has an extra killer ingredient – continuous roaring, belting pop music from its own resident DJ.

Somehow Treasure is able to relax and think clearly

in this atmosphere. She drifts through it as if through a peaceful and sheltered glade, selecting tasteful bargains. To facilitate this talent the Mother must, as usual, be positioned correctly – within sight but not within interfering distance. Thoughtlessly I get left behind. Treasure appears from behind a bank of Levis.

'What are you doing,' she snaps. 'You're going to get lost.' She throws herself back into her work. I stagger after her. I hate the hovering, waiting, standing and choosing. I find a lovely pink vest. My waist aches, I have ten-ton legs and my forehead is sweating. This is my normal condition in large stores throbbing with noise now that I am approaching bus-pass age. But I cannot rest. The entire store is chair-free.

At last we reach the mile-long queue for the fitting rooms. Still not a chair in sight. Treasure has skillfully collected armfuls of chic and modestly priced garments, the music booms on, the stifling heat persists and I have had it. Boiling, exhausted and deafened I sink to the floor and sit down in the queue. I hear the distant voice of an assistant.

'What's the matter with that woman?'

Treasure is horrified. She hisses instructions. 'Get up Mum. What are you doing?' Her mother is becoming a liability. Shop assistants rush forward offering chairs and drinks. They propel me towards a large fan and seat and fetch a glass of water. I am ever so impressed. While working like slaves in this hell-hole they are still able to be pleasant. So is Treasure.

'Let's go Mum,' says she. 'I don't mind. I'll put everything back.' A terrible prospect. It would mean the entire expedition being undertaken again. Bravely I wave her away.

'Go and try them on.' She flits in and out of the fitting rooms to check on my state of health. An elderly, wilting mother must be something of a burden.

Grandma has long been aware of such difficulties. Months ago she rang up in a panic. 'A woman of fifty-nine has just given birth,' she roared rather tactlessly to the Gardener, who happened to pick up the phone. 'For God's sake be careful.'

She was right to advise caution. Had this woman considered the future? Is she prepared for Top Shop at seventy-four with her Zimmer-frame and daughter? This should be a key question when planning motherhood late in life. And here am I, already weak and vapourish at fifty. At least I have my new pink vest. Soon, revived by the chair, fan and water, I am able to sit upright. Treasure has chosen. It is over.

On our way home, united by adversity, we stop in a café for chicken, mayo and salmonella sandwiches. Treasure is most solicitous. We reach home alive with our holiday wardrobe. This is definitely one of our more successful outings.

Glastonbury Slaves

Treasure wants to go to Glastonbury again. But a normal weekend in this hellish venue is no longer adequate. She's done the weekend, now she wants the whole week – seven days employed to pick up rubbish. Treasure has paid sixty pounds to the Glastonbury extortionists, and when she's slaved for seven days, they will kindly give her the money back. *And* she gets free accomodation and staff lavatories.

Naturally she has planned this without asking her mother's opinion or permission. She is thrilled to be on the early morning shift, rising at 6 a.m. to gather refuse.

'How will you get up at six?' I ask crabbily.

'Oh we never sleep there anyway,' trills the Treasure.

I see. Four days off school, seven days without sleep, plus loud and ceaseless noise day and night in several dozen acres heaving with youth, drugs and all manner of depravity, and my Treasure rising at dawn in a mist of spliff fumes to gather up dog-ends, needles, diseases,

'You can't stop me. *I AM GOING.*' Treasure's life
is ruined and I am the cause . . . the blot on
her horizon, the crusher of spirit . . .

111

hamburger fragments and heaven knows what other bits and pieces of noxious detritus. I forbid the Treasure to go.

There follows a week of hell. I thought I had known hell before, but I didn't. Now I do. Treasure is demented with fury.

'I am going,' she screams, louder than ever before. 'You can't stop me. I AM GOING.'

The house throbs with hatred. Treasure's life is ruined and I am the cause. I am the blot on her horizon, the crusher of spirit and enterprise. Fury has strengthened Treasure. Her door-slamming threatens the structure of our home. Doors dangle from their hinges, plaster crumbles. Treasure's vocal chords are also under threat. Her voice has dropped an octave and developed a new coarseness. The dog's bowels are weakening.

Then suddenly things calm down. What can have happened? Treasure no longer seems desperate to be a Glastonbury slave. She wishes to go for the weekend only. We have a moment of calm, but then more turbulence. Another frightful problem rears up. Will Treasure be able to sell her ticket? She is too young to pay for Glastonbury. She has just realised that she can get in free with an adult. So can all her friends.

Who is this mystery adult willing to be followed into purgatory by a flock of children? Treasure answers in a vague way. It's a friend of a friend of a friend's mother/father/big brother. How kind of that person. But now Treasure needs to find another mug to work at dawn among the rubbish for flumpence.

112   'I've got to get my money back,' she snaps in a sinister

voice. 'I can't afford to lose that money. If I can't sell that
ticket I'm going to HAVE TO GO TO WORK THERE.'

Then I'll forbid it and we'll be plunged into hell again.

Will she sell her ticket? We are on tenterhooks. Treasure's bank account and our mental health are dependent
on her success. Tense and numerous phone-calls are
essential. We endure several days of stress and anxiety.
At last a result. So and so's friend's friend's friend will
buy it.

We breathe again, the house is calm, the dog's bowels
settle down. Soon Glastonbury will have come and gone.
Treasure is in a sunny mood. She chatters blithely about
the future.

'I'm going to the Womad Festival in Reading,' she
announces cheerily. 'Andrew asked me and I AM GOING.'

In the distance I recognise the gates of hell.

Grandma is soon to visit again. She is sick of Hove. She
cannot even paddle in the sea in this lovely hot weather
because the beach is a range of huge pebble dunes that no
one over forty and unskilled in mountaineering can cross.
This is unfortunate for a retirement resort. Up here in
town she may sit in the sunny garden and relax.

But I will have to tell her about the fire. She is
bound to spot the missing furniture, charred remains
and redecorations.

Luckily the news of my £24,000 insurance claim cheers
her up, but only briefly. 'If only your father had lived to
hear that,' says she glumly. Grandpa would have been
over the moon. Receiving a huge sum of money from the
insurance company would have brought him happiness.

But we must now celebrate this windfall without him. I can now explain the cello, the new computer, the lovely new curtains and carpets to Grandma. And the act of God that caused our fire. Who else could have knocked a picture off the wall, onto a candle, which fell off the mantelpiece and rolled yards across a wooden floor, then under a bed, set fire to the mattress, and all without the flame going out? No human could have managed it.

The New Rule

Late breakfast time. I am in the garden with my coffee, muesli and newspaper, the dog dribbling at my side. The sun is shining. I am in heaven. Suddenly I hear the sound of Treasure. She is bellowing in an urgent tone from the depths of the house.

But I have made a new rule. She is to come and speak to me politely rather than roar from a distance. I will no longer answer distant roaring. Past experience has shown that it rarely indicates an emergency. Treasure has always claimed not to understand the story of the Boy Who Cried Wolf.

I stay in my deck-chair. This is difficult for me after years of subservience and springing to attention, but I manage it.

'MUM, MUM,' screams the Treasure. Can she have broken a limb? Is her bedroom on fire? Recklessly I stick to my new rule. I will not run and pander, I will stay still, responding in a moderate way when approached, addressing Treasure only from a civilised distance. My

Advisors will be thrilled to bits. For a decade they have begged me to behave in this way.

And there is another disadvantage to the distant roaring which strengthens my resolve. It alerts the neighbours to our activities. Thanks to Treasure's piercing and informative screams, they are now familiar with the details of our private life. Ornamented by Treasure's odious vocabulary and perjorative, descriptive prose, these details may seem rather unsavoury.

'Why don't you run out and tell the whole street?' I asked crabbily as Treasure bellowed some intensely personal details about me and Gardener out of the back door last week.

'They already know,' screamed Treasure, unashamed.

Meanwhile, in the house, Treasure roars on. There she is at the spare room window, red with temper and screaming away, wrapped in towels.

'MUM, MUM.' She waves her arms about in a frenzy.

I continue with my breakfast. I give the dog a section of banana. Treasure looks quite healthy. She mouths horrible expletives through the glass and raps fiercely on the window pane. My apparently relaxed attitude is torturing her.

The dog is beginning to cringe nervously. Can we stand up to this torrent of screeching? What else will the neighbours learn about my private life? Have I any secrets left? Probably not. I gaze at the frogs in the pond, a soothing sight.

But Treasure is drawing nearer. She has descended to the ground floor and is now jumping up and down with temper in the kitchen. She is almost within talking distance. Close to apoplexy, she approaches the back door to the garden.

'What's the matter?' I ask pleasantly, cool as anything. 'What do you want?'

'You are *so* horrible,' screeches Treasure. 'I've been calling and calling. You don't care what happens to me. I could have been dead.' She is outraged by the enormity of my neglect.

'What happened to you?'

'I picked up my towel and THREE MOTHS FLEW OUT.'

Return from Glastonbury

Treasure returns from Glastonbury and is ill at once. Luckily Grandma is visiting again and can act as full-time nursemaid. I return from the shops to find Treasure semi-delirious in Grandma's bed. She spends the next few days sweating, shivering or in the bathroom.

No wonder she is poorly. She has just returned from a sixty-acre pit of filth. Grandma and I saw it on the television while Treasure was away. We searched vainly for her little face among the massed rabble but couldn't find her. Never has a television programme inspired such terror. Somewhere out there among the wild, drug-crazed and abandoned masses, our own Treasure was struggling to survive. Perhaps, even as we watched, she lay out of sight, trampled to death by the eighty-thousand dancing Doc Martens and various clogs.

But no. We got her back alive – just. She had lived for four days on mass catering and using communal lavatories, Grandma's personal vision of hell.

118   'Did those cooks wash their hands after going to the

toilet?' asks Grandma, pale with horror. How many million germs were scudding round the cooking pots? Which of those pierced, matty-haired, heavy-booted, roaring, plaguey youths had used the wash-basins/toilets/ tents prior to Treasure? And now she has stomach-ache/ sun-stroke/exhaustion. We know this illness is genuine. Treasure is too weak to answer the telephone and speak to friends, even Delilah.

I drag her to the doctor. She is rather proud of her ordeal. 'I only saw two bands,' she tells the doctor feebly. 'I felt ill and kept falling asleep. I slept through Oasis, the riot, the battle with the police, the madman running through the crowds with a shot-gun, Lemonheads.'

'It's a virus,' says Doctor. This is rather disappointing for me. I had hoped for something on the lines of, 'It's a dangerous Glastonbury-/drug-/squalor-induced disease that will recur with possibly fatal consequences should you ever visit that iniquitous place again.'

Sadly, the cause of a virus is unclear and there's nothing much one can do about it except lay about missing school.

Gradually, as Treasure recovers her strength, she divulges more hideous details. 'I lost Lizzie as soon as we got there, then I couldn't find Andrew, so they wouldn't let me into the Stewards' tent till he got there because people are always pretending they've got friends in there, and he didn't get there till four in the morning. And the food was horrible, even in there.' Treasure looks glum.

Grandma goes paler by the minute. Luckily Treasure, even in her weakened state and lulled by Grandma's ministrations, wisely omits to describe the ninety varieties of drug with which this annual mini-hell is stuffed.

I have had enough of Glastonbury. Next year the Treasure shall not go. If necessary a ball and chain will be applied. Obviously this will be the last resort. I start now by suggesting in a reasonable tone that perhaps, in view of the general filth, the execrable food, rampaging germs, gunmen and assorted maniacs, resulting in exhaustion, depression and illness, and what with exams coming up as well, it won't be a very good idea to go next year.

Treasure looks puzzled. 'Why not?' she asks from her sick-bed.

Sports Day

It takes Treasure some days to recover from her Glastonbury illness. A week passes and she is still not quite herself. Perhaps now that she has glimpsed paradise, ordinary life is something of a disappointment to her. Down there in Somerset for three days she awoke to the cheery song of the drug peddlers. 'Hash for cash,' they trilled. 'Get your morning trip here.'

'Fifteen people offered Lizzie drugs just while she crossed over one bridge,' reported Treasure. 'She counted them.' Luckily these offers were refused. Treasure preferred to spend her money on a new ensemble and bracelets. She swears it. All around her lay acres of shops and stalls, hours of noise, thousands of boys, gangs of friends and no mother. Even the pestilential lavatories hardly marred this perfection.

'Did you manage to get any sleep?' I asked.

'Oh I slept any time,' said Treasure airily, recounting outrageous bedtimes. 'And then on Sunday I started cooking. I don't know why. I just cooked everything. The rice was exploding out of the pan and I just cooked and cooked.'

Naturally she was exhausted upon her return. Almost motionless, she and the Gang lay about the living room. Treasure ate huge dinners and slept like a top.

And then in come some exam results. Treasure is cast out of paradise and falls into a bog of despair. The world has changed overnight. It has filled with enemies and heartless critics, Cs and Ds, cruel regimes and worst of all – the threat of Sports Day.

'I can't run,' sobs Treasure in a heartrending way. 'I can't. I hate it. I'll come last. People will laugh.'

'It doesn't matter if you come last.'

'IT DOES,' screams Treasure, rigid with terror, her brow fevered. 'I can't run. I CAN'T.'

This is a surprise to me. I never imagined that she cared so deeply about sporting events. Always averse to them myself, I now loathe them all the more. They have wrecked Treasure. She cannot muster up even the weeniest shred of confidence.

Sitting at her bedside I deliver a panegyric to Her. I list her achievements, her talents, her delightful qualities, her As and Bs, her admirers. She will not be comforted. The prospect of the 100 metres has finished her off.

I promise to attend Sports Day. I will wear my best frock. I will not embarrass her. I will eat tea and cakes with the other mummies politely and talk in muted tones, and in a flash the 100 metres will be over and everyone will still love her. And couldn't she follow in the footsteps of a number of friends of ours and take pride in coming last?

122   Treasure perks up a bit. She plans my Sports Day outfit

and falls into a presumably tormented sleep. And before we know it, there we are on the playing fields, the sun shines, a mountain of cakes, sandwiches and strawberries and cream lays ready for tea-time.

The 100 metres draws near. Surprisingly, Treasure doesn't seem to care. She approaches the starting line smiling. Bang. Off go the contestants. Treasure runs along, chatting, as she races, to the two girls on either side of her. Her shoe falls off. She continues cheerily. She comes third from last. She ties her laces to her friend's shoe and both fall over repeatedly, rather annoying Headmistress.

The desolation of the days before has gone. Just like that. Treasure seems to have adjusted once again to our mundane life in town. Her life is something of a roller-coaster. I find the rides rather exhausting.

Sudden Storms

'Can we go to some exhibitions together?' asks Treasure pleasantly. 'If I go with a friend I might not concentrate.'

This is a startling request. Treasure rarely asks to go somewhere cultured with her mother. I research possibilities at once and soon approach Treasure waving an events guide.

'Look, what about the Impressionists exhibition?'

'All right,' says Treasure glumpily. Only minutes have passed since her initial request, but she has already lost interest. Foolishly ignoring this development I prattle on. 'Wedgewood or the Impressionists?'

'Anything,' snaps Treasure, staring fiercely at the television.

'We could go on Sunday.'

Treasure grips the arms of her chair, her knuckles white. 'Would you mind leaving me alone.' She can bear no more. She speaks through gritted teeth. 'Just go away, basically.'

Were I to persist with this topic the Treasure's mood

could easily change from charming to vile in the wink of an eye, as it often does. We will be on the roller-coaster again. Anything can trigger this Jekyll and Hyde effect – an eager mother, the sight of a French text book, the disappearance of a key or T-shirt, or nothing at all. Treasure is on a minuscule fuse and may detonate at the slightest disturbance. We are all on tenterhooks. The dog hates it. It cringes under the table.

Soon Treasure returns to her room. Suddenly we hear a wild burst of screaming and wailing. She comes thundering down the stairs. 'My history notes have gone. You've moved them,' she roars wildly. 'Why have you stolen them?'

Perhaps the Treasure needs a snack. She has not eaten a crumb today. I am grabbing at straws here, but apparently a great wodge of food in the stomach tends to have a calming effect.

'Would you like some dinner?' I ask. It is dinner-time, I am having some, this seems a fairly harmless request, and I know nothing of the history notes. I can offer little else in the way of help.

'No,' roars Treasure like a foghorn. 'Leave me alone.'

I am advised that in such situations one must remain calm. The storm will blow itself out, the notes will reappear, the Impressionist's exhibition will once more seem appealing, the dog will uncringe.

'Don't let things escalate,' say my Advisors strictly. I shall ask them to come and stay for a week. Then they can observe that we don't have escalation, no build up, no visible cause, just sudden eruption, fairly near the top of the Richter scale.

Treasure stamps back to her room. Suddenly the phone rings. She answers it. The sound of merry laughter tinkles down the stairs. Soon we hear Treasure clomping back again. Which Treasure will it be? Witch or fairy? Has the telephone worked its magic?

Yes. Treasure speaks in a normal tone. 'Guess what. Chloe's Mum has kicked her out. She's gone to live in a squat.'

'I wonder why?'

For a moment we are poised on the brink. Has Treasure noticed the thinly veiled sarcasm in my remark? A slight tremor registers in the kitchen. This could be another flashpoint. The tremor passes. Treasure has milk and biscuits instead. What was it all about?

'Hormones,' mumble my Advisors. 'Low blood sugar. And do you spend enough of the right sort of time with her?' What do they mean? Treasure only spends time with her mother if every friend and acquaintance on earth is occupied elsewhere. I try again, an advance booking, now things have calmed down.

'How about the National Portrait Gallery on Sunday?'

Treasure glowers across her milk. Bravely she tries to control herself. She breathes deeply. 'Will you please stop asking me all these questions?'

I see the storm clouds gathering.

New Regime

Term-time is over, Treasure is on holiday. I am not. I am therefore introducing a new regime. Treasure is to do her own washing, and to collect all crockery used by herself and friends and wash it up. This is, in fact, an old regime which has rather been ignored of late while Treasure struggled with end-of-term exams. I am now reviving it.

We begin with a washing-machine lesson. Time has blotted the last one from Treasure's mind. And now we have a new machine, with different knobs and instructions. She must go through the whole boring procedure again, *and* learn to sort clothes: colour-fast, non-colourfast, delicates. It is too much. Treasure begins to glaze over. I cannot complete my lecture. She just manages to fill the machine, twist the knob and turn it on before she bursts out screaming into the street and away.

The sun is out, the Heath beckons, the picnics, the ponds, the chums. She has missed Part Two: 'Then you take the clothes out, then you hang them up to dry, then you put them away.'

Later Treasure returns, sunburnt and exhausted. But more household tasks await her. Holidays bring with them a larger flood of visitors and more debris. The endless summer days must be filled somehow. The chums must eat, flop and sleep somewhere. And Treasure must empty the brimming ashtrays in her room and wash the past terms' mouldering crockery, before Grandma appears.

I see why she has, until now, recoiled from this job. Wodged in the bottom of each cup is a dense mat of fungal growth which Treasure must somehow remove. But Grandma's arrival is imminent, my fury is intensifying and the pile of festering crockery is now so offensive that even Treasure's guests would be sickened. Soon Treasure is at the sink screaming, 'I'm doing it, I'M DOING IT.' She thrashes about in giant peaks of foaming lather and steam, the overflow is fighting a losing battle and to her left a wobbling mountain of clean crockery is growing. Treasure has always refused washing-up lessons. She is self-taught. But I don't care. She is doing it.

I must now leave Treasure at home alone while I fetch Grandma from Hove. I issue strict instructions. Upon our return not a single dirty cup, not the slightest whiff of cigarettes, is to remain. Our home must be clean and fragrant. This objective will be made easier by Mrs Clarke, who I have paid to clean the house to Grandma's approved standard.

But once in Hove I receive a dramatic phone-call from Treasure. 'Ring me back,' she bosses from the payphone which I cleverly installed. 'It's very urgent. My money's running out.'

Whatever can it be? I ring back at once.

'I've had a good idea,' says the Treasure. '*I'll* do the housework. You can pay *me*. Why can't I do it instead of Mrs Clarke? I'm on holiday. I need money.'

I am shocked. Treasure's suggestion is entirely without moral principle. It reeks of nepotism and requires the sacking, without notice, of a hardworking and innocent employee. And it has slipped the Treasure's memory that she promised to do two lots of washing up per week in exchange for pocket money.

I turn down Treasure's job application.

'Why not? Just tell me why not?'

I cannot. I am phoning long-distance from Grandma's phone and frittering her pension. And it would take too long. Treasure has cleverly turned my regime into a complex industrial dispute, mixture of wages for housework and free market economy. If terms are not met she may strike. Will we return to find a sparkling clean kitchen?

No.

An efficient regime needs a ruthless dictator.

Morals

Treasure has been at the bleach bottle again. She goes for it at the beginning of each school hols. Last year's ordeal has not deterred her – the lemon coloured straw hair, the near expulsion from school, the squillion pound hairdresser's bill to dye it back in two stages to its original light brown. Still she must tamper with it again, very quietly in the bathroom while I am not looking.

'It's only Sun-In,' says she, once her hair is safely murdered. 'It'll be like Delilah's. Hers is nice isn't it? You like hers don't you?'

'Yes.' Delilah's hair is subtly shaded, as if the summer sun had gently brightened it. But unlike Delilah, Treasure needs to be dead certain of a striking result. She cannot relax and wait for the potion to take effect, and if the blond streaks don't show up within the hour, she applies another vicious colourant. Soon the Treasure's lovely thick shiny brown hair is yellow again. For some reason she prefers blondes.

130   I had my hair done once as a child. It was permed

against my wishes, turned into dead parsley and I looked fifty-five for six months. I have never since dared to tamper with hair, but Treasure is fearless.

So is Rosie. She comes to visit. Her hair, once lemon, is now fluourescent pink. She and Treasure, their heads glowing brightly, sit at the kitchen table together praising each other's coiffures. The dog and I are blinded by the glare.

'It's better, that colour,' says Treasure, gazing lovingly at the pink.

'Yeah. That blonde was really boring.'

I dread that Treasure will now go pink. Beginning of term approaches and she will face certain expulsion. But no! She seems to have learned from experience. That very evening she appears with three carefully dyed experimental strands of her hair, each in a subtle light brown.

'Good?' she asks. 'Look. I'm testing it properly.' This is a staggering breakthrough. Treasure has, at last, read some instructions carefully and followed them to the letter, the behaviour of a model child. Hopefully her efforts will be rewarded. She applies the same method to the rest of her hair, sticking strictly to the rules, but appears later looking rather peaky.

'Look,' she whispers. 'My hair's gone purple.'

Sure enough, her hair is now a strange purplish colour, nothing like the pleasant light brown strands promised by her earlier experiments and the picture on the packet.

There is now only one person who can save Treasure. It is Elaine the Hairdresser, with her emergency highlight treatment for ruined hair. For hours she fights to salvage what remains of the Treasure's coiffure. At last the straw is transformed, the hair chic and gleaming. This is an epic process and naturally costs half a mortgage. Materially and spiritually this is a wretched episode and demonstrates some depressing truths: obeying instructions gets you nowhere, goodness is not necessarily rewarded and money brings you happiness.

But Treasure still clings to some sort of moral code. She has recently become a blond vegetarian. She swears that both these conditions will be everlasting. I had thoughtfully purchased a mountain of frozen dinners containing meat, to obviate slaving at the cooker and so that Treasure and I might have a constant supply of delicacies, now that we have returned to the harsh world of school. But my hopes and plans are dashed. Treasure rejects all these foodstuffs. She will never eat meat again.

'What about the nice chops I've bought?'

'Don't talk to me about chops.' She shudders with loathing. I cannot enjoy my salami snack in her presence. She sees me not as a peckish mother but as a vulture at a putrefying carcass.

'Well what would you like for dinner? Any ideas?'

'I'm not hungry.' Treasure sweeps from the kitchen.

Out come the dreaded rice, pasta, cheese and tuna fish, our staple diet for the years to come. According to my Advisor, this is inadequate. Treasure requires four varieties of nutrient, a quantity of each to be consumed every day, if she is to survive as a vegetarian and avoid the fainting, nausea, stomach cramps and general weediness experienced during the last vegetarian period two years ago. A vile temper also featured.

It now features again. Treasure comes home ravenous after a day avoiding meat to find Gardener and I just tucking into the first few mouthfuls of a delicious dinner of fish and chips and an *haute cuisine* impromptu sauce. We were not expecting her.

'I want some,' she cries wildly, regressing several years and plunging her hand into my chips. She avoids Gardener's dinner, perhaps made wary by the protective and slightly menacing way in which he is crouched over it. Wisely she concentrates on mine, grabbing at morsels. The dog's manners, comparatively, are impeccable. It whimpers and dribbles away beside us.

I drive Treasure away from the table, ordering her to make herself an omelette. In a fury she battles with it, churning it about in the pan, flings it onto a plate and leaves the room, having cast rather a pall over our charming dinner.

Fortunately she is keen on outings at present. Repelled by the company of her carnivorous and selfish mother and the bits of corpse in the fridge, she is off like a shot at the slightest opportunity.

'I'm going to see A, B, C and D at the market, then I'm going to meet E, F, and G, then I might stay at F or G's house, I don't know yet. I'll ring you up, and will you STOP looking at me in that anxious way. I AM NOT HUNGRY.'

Off she goes, a pallid figure, her hair and body drained of colour by peroxide and iron deficiency respectively. They are rather a good mix and match.

I spend a dreary week, studying nutrition in large text books and trudging round the local health food emporium. An eternity of chopping, mixing and fiddling   133 with tempting and nutritious foodstuffs lies ahead, to ensure that Treasure swallows enough dinner. And just as I have stuffed the larder with pulses, soya products and essential dietary supplements, Treasure returns from an outing. She is in a surprisingly pleasant mood.

'I've just seen Andrew,' says she. 'We went all round the market and we had such a good time and he bought me a hamburger because I was so hungry.'

'A hamburger?'

'And I'm not a vegetarian any more.'

Noise Nuisance

I am in my neighbour Mrs Perez' garden having tea and cakes in the lovely sunshine with chums. We are trying to relax. Suddenly a terrible shrieking rends the air. It is Treasure on the telephone. She is chatting and laughing in rather a peircing way with the window open.

Mrs P and her chums find this amusing. I am mortified. We are three gardens away and still there is no escape. I bellow back at the Treasure, 'Stop that dreadful noise, the whole street can hear you.' Mrs P and chums laugh merrily. Now the whole street has also heard me. We are obviously a problem family and source of noise nuisance, polluting the environment. I am deeply ashamed.

If there is one nuisance that I deplore more than all others, it is noise. Treasure is forever causing it: shouting, dancing, clomping up and down, slamming doors and of course playing music, often the sort with the repetitive beat banned by our government. The noise nuisance is torture and here it is spreading all over the street. And I

135

Suddenly a terrible shrieking rends the air.
It is Treasure on the telephone.

am contributing to it by screaming instructions across the gardens. I thought I had noticed some cold glances from neighbours.

'My mother has been to stay,' I informed one neighbour the other day.

'I heard,' said she, smiling politely. Then we have the dog barking, Treasure's violin practice, my cello practice and the piano banging on. What luck that the neighbour is still smiling.

I heard that years ago a gentleman in New York, maddened by the sound of a neighbouring radio, shot its owner dead. Perhaps Treasure, Grandma, the dog and I should try to modify our behaviour, but this is a trying time for us. Gardener is making two patios in the back garden. He needs to hammer at rocks and use stone-cutting equipment.

Naturally, this puts Grandma's nerves on edge and sets her bellowing, which has a knock-on effect throughout the house. Her dreams of sitting in a lovely, peaceful, sunny garden have been shattered.

There is only one advantage to the noise nuisance. I am easily able to eavesdrop. Whatever vital knowledge I cannot glean from Treasure through normal channels – conversation, question and answer – I can, with little effort, learn from the shrieking phone conversations. I simply sit quietly in my bedroom or on the landing and there it is – a non-stop flow of information.

'And they were up all night making this tape so I fell asleep on a bean-bag for an hour and when I woke up there was nobody there! Then I found them downstairs in the kitchen talking and now I'm knackered.'

137

Then I can ask Treasure in a casual way whether she had enough sleep while out visiting.

'Course I did,' she snaps. 'What's the matter with you? They stayed up all night but I slept for hours.'

I hear her again at midnight, clumping across to the loudly ringing phone. 'You can't come round,' says Treasure, in what she thinks is a whisper. 'My mum's having a bit of an epi downstairs.'

I imagine she is describing some sort of seizure. It has been one of those hot and sultry days when the mess, visitors and noise has been peaking and I have been obliged to shout instructions. Treasure presumably learns noise nuisance from her mother, who learns from her mother, who probably learnt from her mother. Will I be able to break the cycle? Or will the neighbours have live entertainment all summer?

Summer is obviously a difficult season. Now that exams are over, it is the time for throwing children out. Treasure comes home with heartrending reports.

'X has left home. Her mother's so nasty to her/ Y's mother has thrown him out. Isn't that horrible? His Mum says he's got to pay rent. Isn't that disgusting?'

For Treasure's older friends, the crunch has come. Exams are over and a world of opportunity awaits them. It waits in vain. They are not keen to enter it. Treasure and her chums seem to have gone haywire. They have lost track of time.

Followed by the usual cohort, Treasure has taken to coming home at 3 a.m. for snacks. She clatters about in the kitchen, cooking away, and then, as the weather has been hot and sultry of late, she carries their meal into the garden, where everyone may sit, chatting, eating and generally carousing as if it were lunch-time, just outside Grandma's open window.

I hear a dreadful roaring noise. Grandma has reared up at her window and is screaming abusive instructions at Treasure's groups of revellers. This is the third consecutive night of 3 a.m. snacking, and the loudest. They are getting into the swing of things – lively nights, unconscious days, and it has slipped their notice that when they arrived here the house was in darkness and its residents asleep.

This time I am too exhausted to go downstairs and shout. I lie in a dull and sweating fury in bed. At last the lunch party is over. It is 4 a.m. I can no longer sleep. But Treasure can. She has collapsed in her bed and is sleeping peacefully.

In bursts her near-demented mother. 'How dare you wake us up three mornings running at 3 a.m.?

Treasure pretends to snooze on.

'Do this once more and you can find somewhere else to live.' I have joined the crew of heartless and disgusting parents that Treasure has often described. She sensibly remains silent. In a few days she is off to Cornwall with a chum. She will need funding. A mother half crazed with exhaustion is not likely to be generous.

No wonder it is throwing out time, and not just in London. This penchant for night-life is nationwide. I receive a desperate call from my cousin in the north. The daughter is playing up, mixing with rockers, painting her nails black and dragging home disreputable chums for midnight lunches. And she's crashed the car at a pop festival. Cousin is exhausted. She must get up at seven and go to work.

The Daughter is not keen to follow her example. She is searching for jobs in a desultory way, rather as they do down here. There are, after all, better things to do. All over town, every week day, dozens of houses are left empty while the parents are out toiling away at work. Treasure and her friends may flop about in them, feeding, resting, making a noise. Then they can do the same all night while the parents are asleep. And if they go clubbing or wander the streets all evening, they need never see an adult all holidays.

I am sick of all this. I accost Treasure one sunny afternoon as she flops about snacking after a day in the park.

'What about some tidying?' I nag. 'What about a job?'

Treasure is stunned. I am the cruel overseer with the whip on a slave ship. How otherwise would I expect her to work?

'I've been working hard for FIVE YEARS,' she screams. 'I deserve a rest.'

'What? Where?'

'AT SCHOOL.'

The jaw drops open.

Rows

I have had a row with Gardener. Treasure is thrilled. She
senses a drama, and someone other than she is receiving
a drubbing. This is a novelty. To her mind my friendship
with this chap is tremendously dull. It is years old and
uneventful. We eat dinner, we watch the telly, we do not
drink or smoke. We are a stodgy pair and tedious beyond
belief. Sometimes we go out and visit similarly dull and
elderly friends. And now we have had a row about the
garden improvements.

Usually it is Treasure who has the rows. She has always
been the flighty one.

'Her relationships are tempestuous,' said Headmistress
when the Treasure was three and had battled long and
fiercely over some playdough and a frilly dressing-up
frock. Things are much the same now, except that Treasure is much bigger and the tempests cause uproar. A row
with a friend means misery in the home. If the friend
has been horrid to Treasure, then Treasure is horrid to
her mother, her Grandma, the dog and the Gardener,

if he is about. Why not? What else are we there for? When Treasure is upset she introduces a new code of conduct. She may behave vilely, but everyone else must be pleasant back.

'Be nice to me,' hisses Treasure, poised like a snake. 'You've got to be nice to me. Please come here,' she commands in a menacing whisper from a darkened corner. 'I need to talk to you.'

'What's the matter?'

'I've *got* to use your phone.' For a row the upstairs payphone is inadequate. A row can take hundreds of ten pence pieces. 'Unbar your phone. *Please.*'

I sometimes allow a brief row call after 6 p.m. Allowances must be made. 'I can't help it,' moans Treasure after a particularly foul bit of behaviour. 'I'm very upset.'

Grandma retreats to her bedroom in despair, moaning, 'Will I live long enough to see her be kind to her mother?' This is a common refrain. My row with Gardener is a welcome relief to Treasure. Grandma can see that there are other irritating people about.

I have to admit that Gardener has been playing up lately. He is a pleasant enough fellow, but has a tendency to digress. He has a brief dig or trim, but then must be off writing a poem or looking at the full moon or odd cloud formations.

'It's a noctiluscent cloud. I haven't seen one since I was twelve,' says he dreamily, and floats away.

Our garden is a wasteland. Gardener has given no date for completion. How can he? Another odd cloud may appear, a poem beg for expression. An interesting book or Open University programme may take his fancy.

142

Or he may need to rest or arrange things at home in attractive clusters – little bits of twig and dried leaves, a plastic wrapper, a cork.

Meanwhile, there is hardly an inch of patio on which Grandma may sit. Over the last few months, between poems and clouds, Gardener has removed it stone by stone. Naturally there has been tension in the garden. Grandma's and Gardener's methods often clash. And the dog no longer has a lavatory. It dislikes using a barren wasteland. It likes a patch of grass secluded by shrubs. Only the Treasure can keep out of this. She sunbathes on the roof.

Naturally Grandma finds it difficult not to criticise my choice of male friend. 'He's your friend,' she drones. 'There must be something nice about him. If you like him I won't say anything.' She wrinkles up her face in a pained way and glowers into space. 'I might say too much.' She has two dreams: one, that Treasure will be kind to her mother, and two, that I will marry a kind and solvent man. She has all but given up hope. Day after day the Treasure screams about and the Gardener diddles about. Grandma is blind to their charms. The strain of the bleak and ruined garden is beginning to tell.

Treasure is thrilled to find one of my friends in the dog-house. She and Grandma tend to gang up and criticise him. There is nothing like a common enemy to bring people closer together.

Luckily we are going away. There will be no Grandma, no Gardener and no dog, only Treasure, Delilah and me in Spain. And I need not even worry about the dog languishing unloved in a kennel. It is going to stay with the builder who restored our home after the fire and is dead keen to foster it. Grandma will be down in Hove supervised by neighbours, Gardener will be able to bang about the garden undisturbed. This holiday comes in the nick of time.

More Holidays

We have a relaxing few days at the beginning of our
holidays. Treasure and Delilah seem rather lethargic.
Perhaps they find the baking heat of southern Spain
debilitating. They rise at two in the afternoon, have a
leisurely breakfast, reach the beach by tea-time, arrange
themselves attractively on sun-loungers, apply lotions
and puff at Delilah's poisonous cigarettes.

Gradually the beach fills with youth, carrying ghetto
blasters, volley-balls and more cigarettes. The air fills
with fumes and brutish noise. Gangs of sun-tanned boys
bound in and out of the waves, muscles rippling, brandishing surf-boards. Purgatory-*sur-mer*.

Luckily I need not stay here. I have grown-up chums in
a holiday home up the road. I visit them daily for tea and
biscuits by the pool, leaving the girls on the beach – two
reclining chimneys, surrounded by lolling youths, grilling
in the sun.

It exhausts them. They can just manage an evening
stroll and meal before retiring to their room to fiddle

about. They try feebly to locate the disco, but fail. Delilah seems to lack incentive.

Soon, despite lashings of Factor 25 sun block and parasols, they are grilled lobster red. In intense pain they struggle out to dinner. The kind restaurant proprietor advises us. Soak some large cloths in a bucket of iced water and vinegar, says she, and slap it onto the affected areas. These areas are extensive. We spend several evenings doing this in our hotel room. The week passes pleasantly. It is uneventful except for the rock band practising next door.

Risking tinnitus, Treasure and Delilah loiter close to this sound. They soon locate the musicians, then the discos, the night life and the Port and indigenous pits of depravity. Now that they've found it all they must be off raving at once. Tonight.

Discos in this resort begin at one in the morning and end at dawn and there is no such thing as bedtime. This suits Treasure to perfection. It is a format that she has been aiming for over the years and has tried hard to attain at weekends. Here she may do it – diddle until midnight and then whiz off into the night, leaving the elderly chaperone in bed with a book.

But I cannot sleep, what with the sweltering heat, the rock band still practising, the mosquitoes screaming about and my charges out God knows where. Will I ever see them again?

I lie sweating till 3 a.m., then creep down to the hotel reception. Is their key still there? Are they still out? Yes. I return to bed. I must sleep. If I am to be up and about in the morning dynamically contacting the

There is a festival in our Spanish holiday
resort – parades, dancing, flowers . . .
Treasure and Delilah are not impressed.

emergency services, Interpol and the drugs squad, then I must preserve my strength.

At 5.30 a.m. I wake up again. Once more I descend trembling to reception. The wretches are still out. I am having stomach problems. Nine o'clock. I wake and descend again. This is it, the last chance. Time to call upon my friends to act as translators and alert the police. I descend the final flight, I approach the desk. Are the keys still there? Are the treasures back? Or have they been snatched from El Puerto, bundled onto a yacht and whipped away into the white slave trade? I am losing control of my stomach and legs. I can scarcely reach the reception desk.

But the little toads have at last returned. In fact here they are, staggering down the stairs. 'We just got in,' says Treasure cheerily. 'First we went to the disco by the Port, the we met those English boys from the beach, then we went to another open-air disco, then we all sat on the beach and now we're going to have some breakfast.' My relaxing holiday ends here. Theirs is just beginning.

There is a festival in our Spanish holiday resort – parades, free distribution of fruit and flowers, dancing and horse-riding display. Treasure and Delilah are not impressed. They lie inertly in their room or on the beach. Nothing takes their fancy.

But I am very keen on horses. I urge them just to come and watch a little snatch of clever riding, a small outing with my friends, just to be civil and say hallo. Charitably they agree to come. The horse show is opposite El Puerto, area of throbbing night-life and discos. If Treasure and

Delilah are bored by the riding, they can always nip across to a bar, sip drinks, toss their long blond hair and wait for Mummy.

Then another obstacle rears up. The riding is to be held in the bullring.

'How disgusting!' shouts Treasure. 'I'm not going. I am not going to a bullring. How *can* you go in there. You don't deserve to live.' Delilah agrees. No bull fighting is to take place, but both refuse to even enter the site of such barbarity. On principle. They will only sit outside on the wall. Both sneer as I enter, but I must go into the murder arena because I've arranged to meet my friends there.

It is dreadfully noisy inside. There are my friends waving away on the stone seats which encircle the ring. Sophie, a school friend of Treasure's, sits obediently next to her Auntie. She is also on holiday in this resort.

'Where's Treasure?' they ask eagerly. 'Look, Sophie's here.'

I must break the disappointing news that Treasure and Delilah cannot come and join us. Their moral principles will not allow it.

'Rubbish,' shouts the bossiest friend. 'I'll get them.' She strides to the exit. Will there be a stand-up battle over animal rights, offending the friend and surrounding Spaniards? I follow closely, ready to step in and avert bloodshed, but surprisingly Treasure gives in. The lure of Sophie, lack of bulls and steamrollering friend does the trick.

But Treasure was right. Even without the traditional blood and gore the place is a hell-hole. Five very dull clowns are fiddling about in the ring. On and on they

149

go, round and round, falling over and blowing little trumpets. And round again. And again and again. The stone seats are boiling hot and brutal, the noise deafening and relentless, the whole place stifling. How many more minutes can we endure?

Then at last a horse and rider appear. The horse does little steps sideways, this way and that, little steps forwards and backwards, while a complex quadruple bit mashes its foaming mouth to pieces. And what for? We are all bored to death with the little steps and worried about the wrenched mouth and dribbling foam. I am desperate to get out. If only I had sided with the Treasure and adhered to her moral principles.

We manage to leave early on some trumped up charge: 'I have promised to phone my sick mother in Hove.' This is becoming a sterling excuse. It has usefully replaced. 'I must return to my helpless child.'

We arrange to meet the friends later in a quayside restaurant. Another disaster.

'You look lovely,' says my friend innocently to Treasure as we arrive. Treasure grunts a dull reply. If only she would respond pleasantly to adults as Sophie does, then life would be a walkover. She cannot. Treasure is finding it difficult at present to differentiate between being amusing and being insolent. And laden with paranoia she interprets my friend's harmless compliment as heavy sarcasm. Through Treasure's jaundiced eyes, 'you look lovely' means 'what an odious-looking child'.

Perhaps the bullring episode has soured her view of life. Our meal at the quayside is very tense. Treasure and Delilah become so amusing/insolent that we dismiss them early to wander the bars and discos alone. Sophie stays with her Auntie.

I question Treasure and Delilah later. Why did they have to be so rude at table?

'Rude?' Here are two angels with large blue eyes, unjustly accused. They form a team. They stare wide-eyed, denying facts, contradicting truths, both born to mystify, and I have come unprepared. I should have obtained written statements signed by several witnesses but forgot. I am at a crippling disadvantage – one elderly, slightly worn and relatively unsuspecting mind against two razor-sharp new ones.

Soon a different story emerges. *My* friends were rude to Treasure and Delilah – two young innocents set upon by a gang of fascist elders, when all they'd been doing was trying to enjoy themselves.

'Say sorry,' weeps Treasure. 'Say sorry for believing *her* instead of *me*.' But my friend is a grown-up headmistress. She surely cannot be lying. And I saw Treasure and Delilah sulking, swaggering and sniggering with my own eyes. Or did I? Were they just fighting a righteous battle against a gang of cruel insensitive grown-ups? I will never know. Truth is obviously in the mind of the beholder.

But my friend was right about Treasure's appearance. She does look lovely for the most part. So does Delilah. They make a stunning pair. However, I am occasionally shocked by Treasure's holiday outfits. It is boiling hot here and clothing is generally scanty, but her style seems rather saucy – the usual bum length skirt yesterday and a little waistcoat, close-fitting and low cut with a zip-up the front, and in case this was not quite bold enough, she has

151

stuffed a packet of Silk Cut plus lighter into her cleavage. I think this rather lowers the tone of her ensemble.

The streets ring with wolf whistles. Treasure and Delilah count forty-six on the morning of the Silk Cut accessory. They are not displeased.

Why not? Why are they not complaining fiercely of sexual harassment and demanding the freedom to express their sexuality in peace? This must be a post-feminist backlash.

I have spoken to Mrs Perez about these rather provocative outfits. Her own treasures used to wear them a few years ago. She says that the youth of today have a different atitude towards sex. They are careless of all opinions except those of their peers. Who cares about the gawping, leering throngs of elderly or boorish men, or the fears of a prudish and archaic mother? Treasure is fearless. What rapists? What kidnappers, muggers and psychopaths that her mother twitters on about? Treasure and her friends can quell them with a sharp telling off or mouthful of witty abuse.

No wonder they dare to dress boldly in a sunny holiday resort. What is the odd continental groper or leerer when compared to the thugs, pimps, muggers and heavies of our own Camden and Holloway streets?

Our holiday continues, but it is impossible to supervise Treasure and Delilah's whereabouts at all times. Even the sunny beach can be hazardous. I allow them to stay there alone and they stay forever. Eight o'clock, nearly dinner-time and they are still out. What are the little minxes up to? I trail back up the promenade to spy. There is the area favoured by youth. I spot the noise and ciggy fumes and sprawling patches of youth crowded round the ghetto blasters. Treasure and Delilah are not in these groups. Night is falling, I wander the beach, searching. Suddenly I hear distant squealing noises. They sound familiar. There are Treasure and Delilah jumping around in the waves with Boys, and here is their grumping mother come along to spoil everything.

We totter on to the end of our holiday. Before we leave, we had decided, we must try a sangria. But tiffs and sulks and circumstances intervened and we never had one.

Shortly after our return home I hear that Delilah and Treasure loved their holiday. They chattered away to Delilah's mother, who reported back to me.

'I hear they had a great time,' says she. 'Thank you very much.'

Is Delilah's mother sure they weren't fibbing? Absolutely.

This must have been a successful holiday.

The Dog's Eyeball

The dog has an eye ulcer. It must have an operation. If there is one thing I hate to contemplate, it is an eyeball operation. I collect the dog after its fearful ordeal. Even after my most dreadful imaginings, it gives me a shock. It staggers from the surgery with a blank, blood-red eyeball and stitches. Where is its eye? I may faint. The dog's nurse and receptionist are quite cheery about its hellish appearance.

They explain. It's eye is covered by a third eyelid. 'It's not as bad as it looks,' they say merrily. 'It doesn't hurt.' They are lying, I know it. Who could feel pleasant with an extra eyelid sewn up over their eyeball? I leave the surgery crying with my tortured dog.

And worse is to come. Drops must be put into the eye. But how? I cannot even look at it without fainting and wailing. I summons Gardener. Luckily he is able to face the eyeball without flinching. He must now visit three times daily to apply the drops. This is saintly behaviour and the dog and I are very fond of him.

After three days I am able to look boldly at the eyeball and, under Gardener's instructions, apply the drops myself. Treasure still cannot enter any room if the dog is in it. 'Erk,' she screams in a heartless way, 'get her out of here.'

The dog must also wear a plastic upside-down bucket collar to prevent it scratching and blinding itself. It crashes about the house, desolate and unattractive. These are desperate weeks. Ostracised by its affliction and spurned by Treasure, the dog blunders around in its bucket, Treasure lives a wild and mysterious life and Grandma and I live on a high anxiety plateau. This rather negates any beneficial effects of our holiday.

Naturally, this illness has brought the dog and I closer together. People are becoming worried about our relationship. I talk to the dog about this and that and allow it onto my bed.

I don't care. The dog is an essential part of our household. It is a calm and soothing presence and is never bad-tempered – unique qualities in our house. I shall continue to look after it in what may be seen as a sickening way. To other dog owners, I am normal. I mention, while out walking with Sylvia and her dog, that I am considering a hot water bottle for the dog's stomach. She is not at all shocked. Her dog has one already – a fur covered panda with staring eyes. But her cat voluntarily cuddled the dog and kept it warm, so the glaring panda was never needed.

These little chats about dogs are tremendously relaxing. I only have them on the Heath – part of a separate life, 155 an escape from the sometimes tense state of play in our house. There are many women wandering about the Heath, refugees from the kitchen or home squabbles. I once met one going round and round a particularly charming wooded area with her two red setters. She had cleverly nipped out before Christmas lunch, but could not bring herself to go home again. Perhaps she is still there, living in a secret hut. Hopefully someone else was basting the turkey.

This is the perfect place when one is feeling dreary. Last week in a sour mood, I came across a lady feeding blue-tits with breadcrumbs. Scores of them fluttered out of the woods and even ate out of her hand. They have learned to whiz out when they see her coming, at any time of day. Then we had a chat about wildlife and her dog's kidney problems. It is a pleasant change to be surrounded by blue-tits, dogs and trees. Of course the Heath has its grimmer side. Certain areas have to be avoided – the patch where someone leaves cooked peas and carrots, (always only peas and carrots) and someone else has been hurling swathes of spaghetti onto the lawns, apparently for the larger birds. She cooks it up at home, so I hear, huge vats of it, and hauls it to the Heath in plastic carrier bags. It is not as entrancing as crumbs for blue-tits and looks rather odd on the grass.

Treasure in Paradise

We are at last going to Ikea. We need lamps, glasses, cupboards, blinds and candles. Our home is in disarray and must be smartened up. To Grandma, who is moving here from Hove, it is something of a come down in the world. She feels she has moved from palace to tenement building.

But most important of all, Treasure has nowhere to keep her knickers. Rosie has smart knicker drawers from Ikea, which makes it something of an imperative that the Treasure has some too.

For months I have fought against this shopping expedition, but now a colleague is also desperate to go. She has no car and longs to be driven there. And she knows the way and promises to navigate. I am only prepared to make this journey with the help of a skilled navigator to guide me to the North Circular road, through endless miles of supermarket estate, to the hidden exit with a tiny signpost that leads to the secret Ikea car park. Alone, I would have whizzed past it and on, round and round forever searching, but Navigator spots it, sharp as a tack, and we plunge off the North Circular, into a maze of side streets and mystery roundabouts leading to warehouse world. We arrive in the wrong car park behind a monster shed. The shed is our destination. It is Ikea.

Throughout this drive Treasure has been in a jolly mood. Once inside she becomes even more animated. Her eyes shine, she darts about, longing for everything. Were we to win the lottery, we could holiday here: spending, measuring, snacking, spending and using the sparkling Swedish lavatories.

Navigator is also in heaven. She fills her trolley in a carefree way and compares purchases with Treasure. As our trolley fills I begin to feel rather hot and weak. Do we need these candles, vases, flower pots, cushions and chocolates that we never came for?

'Look, look,' Treasure calls and points. 'A futon, only £89!'

I refuse to buy one. Somewhere, thousands of pounds away, there must be a limit. And happily, Navigator does not recommend a futon. She has had one and she knows. But Treasure can cope with this deprivation. She has spotted another and another and another neccessity.

'Look, there's Rosie's cupboard, but I like these more, and this desk.'

'You wanted drawers.'

The Treasure glares at me with scorn. 'I need a desk for my homework. You're asking me to choose between my work and my knickers, and I choose my WORK.'

Obviously both items fulfill a fundamental need. We face a stark choice between academic failure and domestic chaos. Luckily the desk is too large to fit in the car. We must face reality. I come to my senses. I have offered Treasure a suitable desk from the second hand emporium round the corner. She has rejected it. Or the large desk-like table in the living room. Rejected. Or my desk. Rejected. Only the shining new desk from Ikea will do. I try a new bargain

'Desk or the new boots,' I say with conviction. 'I can't afford both.'

Naturally Treasure chooses boots. As we arrive home she sighs dreamily. 'If there is a heaven,' she whispers, 'it is Ikea.'

Disappearances

The Treasure is hardly ever here. This is a pleasant novelty. The house is silent, tidy and fragrant. No one smokes, no large impromptu meals are required. The dog and I live on sandwiches and melon. I need never wash up. Gardener and I can have the odd uninterrupted moment together. But soon the novelty wears off. What is Treasure up to? She phones now and again.

'I'm at Delilah's/Dominic's/Rosie's. I'll be back later.'

She appears briefly now and again for clean clothes and snacks. No wonder she prefers to stay elsewhere. There are no parents present. They are all off on holiday. Why stay with your mother and endure vicious house rules – regular meals and sleep, no smoking, mess, noise or insolence – when one can go elsewhere and be free to make a physical and mental wreck of oneself?

Treasure's appearances at home grow shorter. She is beginning to look peaky and rather wild and also tends to be rather demanding.

'I'm really starving,' says she, whirling in with a hunted look. 'What is there to eat?'

I reel off a list of possibilities, but the Treasure rejects them.

'Can we have crispy duck? I really want crispy duck.' And she wants it there and then, at 3.30 p.m., with all the Chinese restaurants closed and her mother unable to whip some up on the spot. She must settle for pasta. What luck that Grandma is away in Hove and unable to see the decline of her grandchild.

The demands continue. 'Can I have a lift to Stoke Newington/fifteen pounds/ your new jumper/ the bed from the spare room taken up to my room for a settee? Now.'

I am rather sick of this. I reprimand Treasure once more for the stench and slum conditions in her room and the constant demands. She is unmoved. She has thought of another demand.

Can she stay in Grandma's flat by the sea-side when Grandma isn't there? Can I give her a lift down when I go to fetch Grandma and leave her there? With two friends? Or three of four?' Or maybe six, plus anyone she happens to meet on the beach?

Naturally Grandma is averse to this plan. She fears an influx of drugs, sex, dog-ends and destruction. She would prefer Treasure to visit with one chum while she is present, like a dutiful grandchild. This is a fairly hopeless wish.

What a pity! The sun is shining, the sea sparkling, but the sea-side holiday is stymied. Treasure whizzes off in a bate, to party. This is, after all, the holidays. Will Treasure ever readjust to normal life?

Meanwhile Mrs Perez' son, the Perfect Boy, comes home from abroad. He has bravely flown home alone and returned to an empty house, leaving Mrs P in Italy. She rings to check on his welfare. He is not to stay alone in the house but is to go and stay with a chum and parents. He does this obligingly, *and* waters the tomatoes first.

I must say I find this rather galling. Although I try to follow Mrs P's example and instructions to the letter, the results are never the same. Mrs P also tells me that as she speaks she is eating delicious juicy plums, drinking freshly squeezed orange juice and lovely wine and that I should have come to Italy. She did invite me.

I could have handcuffed Treasure to my wrist, sedated her heavily and made her endure a dull week in the Italian hills. Or left her here alone. A chilling option.

Perhaps one day, when Treasure is thirty and happily married with two and a half children, dog and hamster, I may go on a relaxing holiday. Dream on.

Friends with Cars

Terrifying news. Delilah has passed her driving test first time. Treasure can scarcely wait to be driven round London. She doesn't have to wait. Delilah turns up on the very day of her triumph to drive Treasure away in the passenger seat, best position for meeting with death and serious injury.

Off they go, smiling and waving. I have forbidden them to attempt the Holloway Road or any other main thoroughfare. It is a lovely sunny day. Will Treasure ever see another one?

I wander about the house, crying softly and waiting for the call from Accident and Emergency. In my youth I drove unaided into a lamp-post in Ruislip High Street, almost scalping myself on the sun visor. My attitude is perhaps coloured by this incident.

Treasure arrives home alive and well a couple of hours later. 'We went round to Andrew's, then we went past Jack's shop, then we saw Chloe on the corner and we gave her a lift to Rosie's, then we went round again.'

This is to be Treasure's new pastime, Driving Around. She chatters on gaily. 'Andrew crashed his car coming down to the Strobe on Saturday. Now all my friends have crashed except Delilah.' This information is intended to reassure me. I sink trembling on to the sofa.

'What's the matter?' asks Treasure. 'It just shows what a good driver Delilah is. And I'm not allowed to talk when she's driving and she won't have the radio on.'

The Drives continue. They soon become more adventurous. I overhear snatches of conversation which suggest that Treasure and Delilah are driving round Marble Arch and Trafalgar Square in the rush hour for fun. Tonight they are driving to a wild venue in the city, a breakthrough outing.

'We've got to be early,' shrieks Treasure, 'because Delilah always gets lost when she's driving.' She rushes out of the house. 'They're waiting for me.' She rushes back. 'Where's the tissues?' she calls briskly, 'Rosie's being sick.' She grabs the tissues and heads for the front door.

'Doesn't Rosie want to come in and lie down?'

'Don't be silly Mummy. We're late.'

Off they go, driving through unknown terrain in the dark, getting lost, being sick, enjoying themselves.

Delilah and Rosie are going on to yet another party to rave until dawn, but I have cruelly forbidden the Treasure to go. She is driven home by Delilah at 1.30 a.m. and left, isolated, a pariah, the Girl-who-may-not-go-for-all-night-drives. Naturally she cannot sleep. She wanders the house in her nightie, peering from windows, opening and shutting the front door, waiting for news of the Drive. She is in limbo for hours, tormented, unable to work, rest or eat.

164

At last she is off at 10.30 a.m., round to Rosie's, but is back in a trice with fearsome news. 'Delilah has crashed her car. There's a huge dent in the side. She's got to pay for it herself. She's so depressed. I've never seen her so depressed. She can hardly speak.'

For one brief afternoon the Treasure is grateful to her mother. Had I not been so heartless and strict, she might also now be intractably depressed or even hospitalised. Perhaps the Drives are over.

Foolish hope. Delilah emerges from her depression and speaks. She merely backed into a bollard leaving the car park.

'It wasn't a real crash,' babbles Treasure happily, 'and next Saturday we're going to Oxford for the day, just for the Drive.'

Shall I tell them about the endless roadworks on the A40? The multiple pile-ups on the M4? Will they care?

The Mutilation

Treasure is in a suspiciously jolly mood. She sits in the kitchen laughing and staring at me in an odd way. She obviously has some vile secret up her sleeve. I notice that there has been a high level of whispering and sniggering over the last few days. Everyone seems to be in on it except me: Selina upstairs, Jane next door, all Treasure's chums.

'Is there anything the matter?'

'Oh nothing.' Treasure splutters and rocks about on her chair. She can scarcely contain herself. 'Do you want to know what I've done?'

'Yes,' I answer grimly. I know she is bursting to tell. In seconds the secret is out. Hideous news. Treasure has had her navel pierced.

'Do you want to see?' she asks eagerly.

'No thank you.'

She displays the area depite my request. I am overcome with nausea. I forbid her to expose her stomach again in my presence. The dog has only just recovered from its eyeball operation and now here is the Treasure mutilated by metal bolts, her stomach done up like Frankenstein's neck. We now live in Hammer Studios. First the dog with the blood-red eyeball and stitches, now the Treasure's punctured flesh and presumably suppurating wound to follow.

It is Sunday. I notice that Treasure is wearing loose clothing. What happens tomorrow with the school skirt waistband and tights wrenching at the laceration? I cannot contemplate it. I am too enraged to shout.

'Why aren't you shouting?' asks Treasure, baffled.

'There's no point,' I say, cold as ice. 'You've done it now. Just as long as I don't have to look at it.' I drive off to lunch at a friend's house, blubbing all the way and remembering the Treasure's once delightful tummy.

Back at home again, strange smells drift through the house. Particular disinfectant has been advised for daubing on to the puncture. Treasure is at least attending to her injury. I find that I am strangely overcome with gloom. Treasure couldn't care. She is unrepentant. She returns from school thrilled.

'Angela Hayley said it looks lovely,' she brags shamelessly. 'She says all catwalk models wear them.' Inspired by Angela's eulogy Treasure takes to prancing about the house in rather brief tops which expose the ghastly piercing. I avert my eyes and shout, she turns her back. We are forever dodging about to avoid a head on confrontation.

These are grim weeks. The remaining summer days are rather soured for me. Out comes the sun and with it Treasure's midriff and mutilation. To her the lump of metal has a jewel-like quality. Her love of piercing never wavers. She comes home with loathsome news.

'Michael Billings has had his eyebrow pierced,' says she. 'He looks wicked.' Treasure fell out with this chap ages ago. He had rather blotted his copybook by charming her mother. In my eyes he was the perfect son-in-law. But now he has disfigured himself she is reviewing her opinion. Someone whose eyebrow could send her mother rushing for the smelling salts is surely to be exalted.

How does his mother manage? Each morning she must face the tortured eyebrow across the table. At least the navel is concealed at meal-times.

'Don't over-react,' drone my Advisors. It could have been the cheek, the chin or the tongue. Or a tattoo, there forever, scarred for life. And at least the bolt can one day be taken out.

Quite right. I am so fortunate.

But I still cannot count my blessings. Treasure is determined to wreck her physical self. She has almost plucked her eyebrows into extinction, her once fresh, glowing skin is often caked with a thick layer of make-up, she *must* meddle with her hair and is now frittering her money on sun-bed sessions. Skin cancer here we come.

Grandma is distraught. Half her family were demolished by cancer and here is her grand-daughter paying for a chance at it. And our cousin from the USA brings dreadful news. Over there, and in Australia, where people of a fair and freckled complexion like the Treasure have been dropping like flies, these poisonous devices have already been banned.

Naturally I pass on their warnings and concerns, but

does the Treasure care? Not a whit. She and another chum, both charred by the sun-bed treatment, sit at table while we, the parents issue terrifying cancer warnings. Both girls smile breezily.

'At least we'll die brown,' says the chum.

I do agree that reasonable discussion is much the best way of dealing with ones' children, but feel that the ball and chain or incarceration in a repressive convent might, in this instance, be more practical.

Choice of Literature

Treasure has a sudden desire to improve her mind. She wishes to buy reference books and classics. Quick as a flash I whirl her to the bookshop before she changes her mind, taking care not to look too keen.

Once within the cultured atmosphere of the bookshop Treasure becomes a stickler for good manners.

'Stop shouting,' she hisses, as I speak to her in hushed tones. She finds my every remark grotesquely embarrassing. I stick to minimal questions.

'What about this?' I point to a suitable book.

'Be quiet.' Treasure is sweating with shame. We may now only use sign language and lip-reading. This makes communication rather tricky. Treasure hovers around in front of the dictionaries, literary notes and revision manuals, demanding assistance but rejecting advice. Eventually a huge pile of academic manuals is acquired. When faced with a difficult choice, she tends to take the whole shop. I am forced to limit her selection. Exhausted by twenty minutes of silent squabbling and choosing, Treasure now needs to relax.

Headmistress will never believe that
I had forgotten the contents of Fanny Hill.

'I'd like some Mills and Boon,' says she, perking up as we approach the till. But this bookshop is rather classy. It does not stock Mills and Boon. However, it does have a huge pile of £1 classics which I often buy impulsively and shovel into the Treasure's bedroom whenever possible. She is not usually grateful. Today I spot *Fanny Hill* in the selection.

'Have that instead,' I say. 'It's just as thrilling as Mills and Boon.'

'And it's better written,' says the assistant. What a charming fellow. It isn't often that a pushy, pressurising mother obsessed with academic success finds an ally in public.

'All right,' says Treasure, bored to death.

I read the first page or two of *Fanny Hill* on my return home. It contains nothing untoward. Will Treasure struggle through the eighteenth-century prose? Probably not. She takes it up to her room. Strangely enough she is glued to this book. She reads it in bed, she carries it about the house. Rosie has a read. Both gloat and snigger.

'What's it like?' I ask.

'It's rather graphic,' says Rosie smirking.

Puzzled by the Treasure's bizarre attack of classic reading I have another look at this book. I read it thirty years ago in my youth, time has blurred my memory and I remember nothing particularly loathsome, nothing more frank and graphic than the problem page of *Just Seventeen*, *Nineteen* or *More*, Treasure's usual literary diet. What a nasty shock to discover page after page of hideous carry on which must surely have soured the Treasure's view of the world. And I am responsible.

172

I cast the book aside and advise the Treasure to read no more. But she is keen to read on. She is, after all, reading a Classic.

'I'm going to tell Miss Harold (Headmistress) that I'm reading it,' says she proudly.

I hide it. Whatever will Headmistress think? I am deeply ashamed. Headmistress will never believe that I have forgotten the contents of *Fanny Hill*. They are, after all, rather striking. Why was it placed among a respectable selection of classics and not on a high shelf out of reach of children and negligent mothers?

Luckily Treasure forgets about *Fanny Hill*, but I am bitterly disappointed by our expedition to the bookshop, which I assumed to be a haven of self-improvement. Things have obviously not changed. The eighteenth century had a charming surface and a heaving pit of filth and corruption beneath, and so have we. I do hope Treasure remains on the surface.

Birthday Surprise

Tomorrow is my birthday. How my birthdays whiz by! Treasure is not as prepared as she was last year. Boys, exams, clothes and raves have rather taken over her thoughts and her wallet. She rushes to Camden Town to buy presents. Soon she rushes back. She tears up the stairs weeping and calls desperately for her mother.

'What's the matter?'

'I've just come home from school, I'm worn out, I go all the way to Camden to get YOU a present and I've got *no money* because YOU cancelled my cheque.' Treasure had forgotten that I had cruelly stopped her pocket money because of some grave misdemeanour committed last week. She screams on. 'I can't do anything. I can't do things that normal people do, I can't go swimming with everyone else, and now I've got to go to WORK. No one else has to. Other mothers won't *allow* their children to go to work. It's embarrassing. You've GOT to give me my money.'

As the Treasure is keen to smoke herself to death, I rather resent funding this habit with pocket money.

'I don't smoke any more,' weeps the Treasure. 'I hardly smoke at all, but I NEED things.'

'What things?'

'Fares, deodorant, make-up. Lots of things.'

I am unmoved. I buy her deodorants anyway and she has enough make-up to cover the cast of *Waterworld* twice. And meanwhile, as we scream away, the sounds float down to Grandma in the kitchen. She too is weeping with temper. 'How can Treasure speak to her mother like that,' she thinks. 'Why is it allowed?' She has never heard anything like it. She is busting to intervene and voice her opinion, but I have forbidden it. She may not join in or revile Treasure. It would not help. Naturally the whole house trembles with suppressed and expressed emotion. What luck that we don't live in Russia where whole families are confined to one room. No wonder people wallow in vodka.

'Please take me to Camden,' moans Treasure. 'I've got to get this job in a café.'

I take her on my way to Sainsbury's, and later, as I plod round the fruit and vegetable area, Treasure appears. She has the job. She has perked up considerably. She even wishes to help with the shopping.

'I'm getting a basket,' says she briskly, 'so I can go round and choose the things I like.'

She returns laden with pies, crisps, pizzas and snacks of dubious nutritional value, but as she is rather frail, pale and twiglike at present, I don't care. She accompanies me round the aisles, selecting more noxious foodstuffs, mostly coated in salt, fat or chocolate, and then she spots the perfume cabinet. There is her favourite perfume, and

175

four pounds cheaper than the duty free. For this reason she must have it. It is snip at £13.95. Had I realised that Sainsbury's sold chic perfume I would have barred the Treasure from entry.

'Take it out of my pocket money,' says Treasure, 'or I can pay you out of my wages.' She continues to help with the shopping, nagging away about the perfume. 'Why not? It's my money, I'll pay for it. I don't see why not.' She pushes the trolley, piles things on to the checkout, stuffs them into bags, and buys her perfume. To the Treasure this is not an extravagance. It is a basic necessity. She would starve rather than smell dull. And what is £13.95 after all? Just a few packets of cigarettes and a couple of cab rides.

I expect my Advisors will drone. 'Why did you allow it? No wonder she helped you with the shopping.'

Although rather disturbed by Treasure's extravagance and growing penchant for luxury goods, I feel I must pre-empt this critique. Treasure's charming and helpful behaviour in Sainsbury's began well in advance of the perfume spotting. And what a charming birthday surprise it was for me. A whole shopping outing without a row.

Bad Fairies

It is Hallowe'en and the Treasure is dressed as a fairy. I have never seen anything so charming. Selina upstairs has helped to create the divine fairy outfit. Treasure is a heavenly vision of innocence in drifting white chiffon adorned with little strands of pretend white flowers, trails of silvery beads and matching head-dress. If only she would adopt this style permanently.

It is years since Treasure went out in a frilly fairy dress. Until now I have never been keen on this kind of slop. What can have happened to me? I never have cared much for frocks and curls and fought non-stop for straight hair and trousers in my youth, a sad time for my mother, cursed with the only child in Ruislip who never wanted to be a bridesmaid.

Perhaps Treasure is reacting against her mother's austerity. She always has – with frocks, Sindy dolls, jewels and perfume, but the fairy dress is perfection.

Imagine my bitter disappointment when the Treasure discards it and reappears in a devilish red and black ensemble instead.

177

'Like?' asks Treasure, swirling about on the stairs.

'Very nice, but what happened to the lovely white outfit?'

'You don't like it.' Treasure's face is thunderous. Her evening is ruined. I do not one hundred per cent love her red and black outfit above all others.

'Yes I do.' But it's no good. Treasure and I both know that the white fairy outfit has stolen my heart. All the more reason for Treasure not to wear it. She stamps off in her devil outfit.

I am often uneasy about the Treasure's choice of fancy dress, or any dress. The next day she is off to another wretched Hallowe'en party. She cannot find her witch outfit and pointed hat, cannot be a devil twice running, and must go as a St Trinian's pupil. She has no choice. Her old school uniform is the only available costume.

With this limited material she whips up a very bold outfit in which the navel is main feature. Attached to the usual metal bolt is a large spray of silver leaves, as if sprouting from the Treasure's middle. This accessory is emphasised by the knotting up of the school blouse and the turning down of the skirt waistband, so exposing Treasure's midriff. But whatever Treasure does to her school skirt, there still hangs about it an odious whiff of respectability. She is forced to reject it and substitute a racy little black leather skirtette instead. She ties her hair into bunches, plasters on one ton of pallid make-up, purple lipstick and nail varnish, adds the knee-socks and usual ten-inch heel clumping footwear, rakish school tie and comes downstairs to give Grandma a fright.

'Good?' asks Treasure, modelling her swizzy outfit up

and down the living room, navel spray sparkling brightly. Grandma looks rather shell-shocked. She manages to smile weakly. She is finding it difficult to deal with the Treasure's increasingly *risqué* outfits and time of departure. I long for the rejected fairy ensemble.

It is now 11 p.m. and Rosie and Treasure are at last ready to leave. Rosie is modestly dressed in a long red worm frock and subtle red horns on a headband. If only Treasure would follow her example. Neither Grandma or I are keen on Treasure wandering the streets dressed like this. Members of the public may not realise it is fancy dress and mistake her for an audacious trollope.

'Can you give us a lift?' demands Treasure. She has learned from past experience that her over-protective mummy can often be coaxed into chauffeuring her to the back of beyond if her outfit is saucy enough and the destination risky.

But this time I won't. It is late, I am tired, Grandma has had a turn and I am not going anywhere. 'No,' I say, and while in this determined mood, I issue further orders. 'And you may not go out in the street looking like that.'

'Well, you should give me a lift then,' bosses Treasure.

'No. Put some jeans over it until you get there.'

Treasure refuses. She is shocked by my rebellion. But should she meet a rapist or murderer she at least knows that I know it will have been my fault, for allowing her out on the streets alone without her chauffeur. She flounces off in a bate. 'I'm going like this,' says she, wiggling down the front path.

Still I refuse to chauffeur and shout horrible warnings

after her. She writhes away, down the street, leaving Grandma and me trembling on the sofa.

But in two minutes the Treasure is back. 'I forgot something,' she shouts, smirking and writhing past the living room door. She bolts up the stairs. She whizzes out again. What can she be up to? I look out of the window into the darkened street. There is the Treasure a few yards along the pavement, struggling into her jeans.

I am thrilled. For once she has done as she is told. She will do it just as long as I don't know that she knows that I know best.

Not Going Out

Treasure is turning over a new leaf. She is to spend more time at home studying and less out raving. This behaviour seems rather modish at present.

'Rosie's stayed in three weekends and David Bradley hasn't been out for thirty-six days!' says Treasure weak with admiration. 'They've got exams.' Exams are months away but she is keen to follow their example. 'Have you noticed I don't go out on Fridays anymore?' she asks. 'Aren't I good?'

'Very.'

'And I'm not going out tonight.' This is her second Friday of voluntary incarceration.

'Marvellous.' I am all for Treasure staying in on Fridays as Saturdays are heavy-duty rave nights. For months I have tried to enforce relaxing Fridays, but with little success and now, at last, it seems that Treasure has paid attention to my advice. Wrong again.

'I'm just going to Paradise with Chloe.'

'I thought you weren't going out.'

'I'm not,' says Treasure. 'I'm just going to say hallo to everybody there and tell them I'm not going. Then I'm coming back. Otherwise I won't see my friends.' She promises to be back by nine-thirty.

Paradise Club is at the other end of the Holloway Road. One trip down this road can bring on intractable depression in the normal human but Treasure is about to nip up and down it for pleasure. She often does this.

'Isn't that rather a long way to go just to say hallo?'

Naturally Treasure finds this question irksome. She cannot bear to answer yet another pointless question from an anchorite mother who knows little of the world. Chloe is waiting, they must leave at once, 'and we're LATE. GOODBYE.'

Off they go, but apparently not out, just down the road to loiter outside some loathsome venue. So long as she remains outside it, and doesn't go in, she is not Out. Obviously *going out* means clubbing, raving or partying until she is more or less done for. A police raid, clubbers dragged from the ticket queue to the cells, the odd scuffle, a dramatic romance or bust-up, murderous noise and damaged ear-drums all rather enhance an outing. In fact they are something of a must. Anything less hardly counts. Especially tonight's brief loiter outside Paradise.

Nine-thirty, the phone rings. It is Treasure. 'I'm back.'

'You are not.'

'I am. I'm at Mark's house.'

Mark lives two doors down the road. She is not out, she is staying in, but two doors away. She stays in/out until ten-thirty. Naturally there must be some sort of contrast between this and a real outing.

182

The real one takes place on Saturday. And now Treasure has adopted the Friday penance of staying in, she must live the Saturday outing to the hilt. Saturday lunch-time she begins preparations.

Late on Sunday she regains consciousness. I ask what she plans to do for the remaining scrap of her weekend. 'I hope you're not going out.'

"Course not. Are you mad?'

How pleasant. An evening in for us all. I begin to plan a meal at a normal meal-time. Treasure fiddles about in her room for an hour or so and then comes floating down the stairs. She heads for the front door. Naturally I have a shout.

'Where are you going? I thought you were staying in.'

'I'm not going anywhere. I'm just going across to Lizzie's.' Treasure stares at me oddly. Has she spotted a large growth on the end of my nose? 'What's the matter with you?' she asks, wrinkling up her face. 'You're being very weird. Why are you being so horrid to me? You ask me to stay in, I say 'Yes, all right' politely, then you start screaming.'

Do we have a communication problem?

The Boyfriend from Hell

Selina the charming tenant is to leave and Treasure is
to move upstairs in her place. This was meant to be a
birthday treat, but it is a little late. This will be vital
when Grandma visits. And she may soon be visiting
permanently. She and Treasure are rather similar in
temperament and cannot be left alone together on one
floor. Our home becomes an emotional hot-house. But
now we will have acres of space – Treasure, her friends
and noxious pop-music upstairs; myself, Grandma and my
friends in an oasis of culture downstairs. This is my plan.
Will it work?

'When can we go to Ikea again?' asks Treasure, already
planning a luxurious penthouse.

'Never.'

'You promised me a futon.'

'I did not.' I have warned Treasure that her large new
chamber and adjoining bathroom will be bleak and partly
crammed with the monster computer. A glamorous salon
littered with futons is not on the cards. She cannot

remember this bit of information. Again and again she forgets it and orders luxury furnishings, dreaming of lounging friends, soft lighting and no homework.

Tonight she has had a chum visiting. I enter her present room. Nicotine and alcohol fumes billow from it. There she is, just visible through the smog, lying on the bed, a glass of moist dog-ends beside her. Perhaps the move to larger premises is a mistake. A cave in the cellar might be more suitable. But it's too late. Selina upstairs has found a new home and the penthouse is to be vacated, just in time for Treasure's birthday. She empties her cupboards, packs her bags and is ever so excited. We begin to move her possessions upstairs.

'Andrew and Delilah are coming to help me move. You go out. I don't mind,' says Treasure rather eagerly. 'We can do it.'

Andrew and Delilah arrive. They tear up to the new premises. I hear no sounds of moving. And Treasure has rather callously banned the dog from her floor. 'Get out,' she roars harshly, 'this is a dog-free zone.' The dog looks rather crumpled. It hangs about on the landing in a forlorn way. I am stunned by Treasure's heartlessness. The move is not enhancing her character.

For some reason I am nervous of leaving Treasure in charge of our home and the dog. There is no longer a charming tenant around to keep an eye on things, hordes of youth will now flock to the penthouse and the dog, already traumatised by the removals, will be isolated and neglected downstairs.

I take the dog visiting with me. I shall be labelled neurotic if anyone hears of this, but I don't care. Still I am unable to relax while out visiting. To the Treasure's immense surprise I am home by midnight. Little moving has been done, as I suspected, and a horrid stench of cigarettes is seeping down through the house from Treasure's appartment. Delilah, down in the kitchen selecting a snack, calls up to Treasure in a casual way, 'You mum's back.'

I hear gasping and scurrying noises from upstairs. Treasure appears looking rather pale. 'You're back!' She is wearing a fixed and mask-like smile of welcome. I retire to bed but hear more scurrying and whispering up and down the stairs. I investigate. A note has been pinned to the front door.

'Dear Andrew, Rosie and anybody,' warns the note. 'My mum is home. Aaarrgh! Do not ring bell or make any noise. Sorry.'

I am not pleased about this note. It is the 'anybody' that I find disturbing. I leave the house unguarded for a few brief hours with its inviting new penthouse and Anybody at Anytime is invited round to play.

The next day I threaten Treasure with eviction. She may not invite hordes of strange clubbers round in my absence, make the house stink of cigarettes or turn her lovely new suite into a slum, otherwise she can *move downstairs again*.

For once Treasure is silent. She tidies her room, goes to bed early and awakes refreshed, her mind clear.

'I really need a coffee table,' says she. 'When can we go to Ikea again?'

186   No wonder Treasure is keen to move upstairs to her

more private appartment and smarten things up. She has a new boyfriend. I think I recognise him as he slides by. He strongly resembles the youth who murdered Treasure's goldfish years ago by adding various shampoos to their water.

'Is that the goldfish murderer?' I ask.

'No,' says Treasure with a rather pink face. 'It's another Dominic.'

I am not pleased. I much preferred the last boyfriend, a pleasant vegetarian with shaved head and spray of small plaits. And can I now safely leave the dog alone with Treasure and her friends? It has a malfunctioning pancreas and one small dollop of butter could finish it off. Suppose the Fish Murderer is aware of this?

I force Treasure to own up. This paramour is indeed the Fish Murderer. But I am assured that he is now a reformed character. He looks back on his callous misdeed with shame. Thank goodness. The charming romance continues.

But not for long. Soon some new faults show up. The Boyfriend is rather weak on punctuality. He is often hours, even days late. He fails to telephone on these occasions to explain his absence. Naturally this distresses the Treasure. Very loud, emotional and everlasting phone-calls take place as Treasure reports to Delilah or berates the Murderer. He is the Boyfriend from Hell. Because of Him, cigarette smoking increases, homework stops, sleep, regular meals and rational thought are no more. Treasure is the victim of a Romance.

And all this in Treasure's sixth year at school with vital examinations looming. Boyfriend could now become the murderer of Treasure's career and all future prospects. School is now a minor irritant in the background. The Romance is top priority.

Boyfriend can even disrupt from a distance. He tends to do this at 1 a.m. when Treasure is slumbering peacefully prior to another arduous school day. I have banned late phone-calls. He ignores my ban. Brring, brring – Treasure staggers from her bed and sleepwalks to the telephone. I rush upstairs to reprimand the caller and Treasure, but she is sitting on the floor entranced.

'It was Him,' says she, looking blessed. The Murderer has rung to declare his love. Alcohol has loosened his tongue. Treasure floats back to bed charmed by this gesture. I am not. It would have been more charming at tea-time and made for a pleasanter day all round. We have had to wait until 1 a.m. for Treasure to be pleasant. If the boyfriend is vile to Treasure, then Treasure is vile to her mother, the dog, Grandma and any one else present.

'I can't/don't want to speak/eat/work/live,' moans Treasure only days later, lying in a concealed heap under the duvet. The Romance is tottering on the brink. Will it and Treasure survive? Will she ever smile again? Everyone plods about the house looking glum. But then the phone rings. It is Him. The sun comes out, people speak again, Treasure's room throbs with pop music. Soon she bounces downstairs.

'It's His birthday,' says she. 'I'm going to make him a cake.'

'*!*!* him,' says Grandma rather crudely. I reprimand Grandma. Criticising the Treasure's beloved will get us nowhere. It will only intensify her love and admiration for the fellow. But Grandma is no good at paradoxical injunction. To calm her down I am forced to speak in Boyfriend's defence.

'He's got exams, he's not well, he's under stress, and he did behave ever so well last week when we took him to a wedding – wore a suit, had perfect manners and sung like an angel in church.' He was the Boyfriend from Heaven. For one whole afternoon.

More Smoking

I notice that Treasure's premises smell almost fragrant during the week. There is hardly a trace of smoke, no dog-ends anywhere, until Friday night. Then three chums come to visit. Within minutes dense fumes clog the top of the house and seep down the stairs.

I scream from an air pocket on the first floor, 'Stop smoking at once.' But Treasure is insulated by noise and smog. She can barely hear me. Soon four sallow, bronchial and reeking figures drift down the stairs. It is Treasure and her chums sliding out of the house, Treasure last. I try again.

'You may NOT smoke in this house.'

'Will you leave me alone,' shrieks Treasure. 'I'm under stress. Can't you see? What's the matter with you? I'm doing exams.' Exams are the blanket excuse for all misdemeanors this year. She grits her teeth and looks forty, a woman upon whom life has taken its toll. 'Just leave me alone.' She sweeps from the house.

I suspect that Delilah is the main source of cigarettes

*Soon four sallow, bronchial and reeking
figures drift down the stairs.*

191

and Treasure is keen to emulate Delilah – same trousers, same college, same blackened, treacle-coated lungs, same early death.

I speak to Delilah's mummy. Startling news. Delilah is not allowed to smoke at home. Or at all. Delilah's mummy is ruthless when enforcing her ban. She screams loud instructions, embarrassing her child and forcing her to walk the streets while smoking. If she can implement such rules, so can I. One day, thanks to us, our children may all have lovely pink clean lungs again.

Luckily my anti-smoking campaign is hotting up. I now have Grandma as an ally. She is fearsome. She stands on guard at the entrance to our home interrogating Treasure's visitors.

'Have you got cigarettes?' she screams boldly at large and hulking youths. 'HAVE YOU? Don't you dare smoke them in front of Treasure.' If she spots a packet she will confiscate them on the spot.

In Grandma's eyes Treasure is still an innocent corrupted by degenerate peers. If left alone she would have grown up vice-free, undemanding, obedient and non-smoking. She fights on to protect her grandchild.

Chloe enters the kitchen on her way to visit Treasure. She had planned to say hallo politely to Grandma, but before she can speak a word, Grandma attacks.

'Pooh!' she roars accusingly. 'Have you been smoking? You stink of smoke.' Perhaps this sort of forthright attack is more effective. My feeble ban and reprimands have got us nowhere. The smoking has continued, dog-ends shower out of Treasure's window into the garden, upsetting the Gardener and spoiling our plans for a delightful wooden bench among the flowers. Treasure will only slouch there with her chums, spraying dog-ends and trampling delicate plants. Inside and out, our home is sullied by Treasure's vile habit.

Meanwhile, Grandma continues her campaign. Defying my strict instructions she crawls up to Treasure's room. Nothing can stop her anti-smoking crusade – not crippling arthritis, not angina, not me. She is determined to inspect Treasure's premises. This is a foolhardy move for a woman with a heart condition but Grandma *will* do it.

A terrible sight greets her. She immediately needs a lie down, tea and the angina spray. I warned her but she would not be told.

There is something oddly familiar about Grandma's behaviour – the forceful opinions, the disobedience, determination and loud noise. I have heard that certain traits can jump a generation.

Elastic Outings

As exams are drawing nearer, Treasure has written out an attractive revision timetable. It is strikingly neat and maps out the coming weeks to the minute. She plans to rise early, work like a demon all through weekends and the Christmas holidays and limit her recreation time.

'And I'm not going out tonight,' says she. 'Good eh? And I'm going to pin my French up all over the walls and keep looking at it.'

Naturally I praise Treasure for her intentions.

'And Delilah's coming round in a minute with a video.' Exhausted by planning the Treasure now needs some time off. She will start the Time-table tomorrow.

It is perhaps rather optimistic. It relies on Treasure's day beginning at 10.30 a.m. and on her presence in the house for long and uninterrupted periods of time. She can do neither of these things. Something about our home repels her. Anywhere else on earth is more alluring: the sunny Heath, the shops, anyone else's house or the street. Because at home the Time-table is waiting for her.

Her days often start in a promising way. 'I'm going to have a bath, then I'm going to tidy up, then I'm doing homework for three hours, then I might go round to Andrew's for a bit.'

I have learned to mistrust these plans. The work period tends to shrink and the mini-outing tends to be brought forward and stretch.

'I'm going to the shop,' shouts Treasure, running from the house as if thrust away by an alien force. The Shop means the beginning of an elastic outing.

Brring, brrring. Treasure rings from a distant High Street. 'We're just getting Andrew's friend a birthday card, then we're coming home.'

She rings again two hours later. 'We're at Andrew's friend's house because he lives near here. We're just waiting for Tom's friend to bring Andrew's jacket round, then we're coming.'

'Come home at once,' I shout. 'What about the Time-table?' But she cannot come home at once. She is now at the other end of the earth, two hours' complex bus and train journey away from home. The Time-table is blown.

At least the elastic outing is punctuated by phone-calls as Treasure reports in from various outposts. But my neighbour Mrs Perez has experienced this ploy from her own treasures in their youth. The frequent calls are to keep the mother calm and happy, says she. They give the impression that Treasure is merely on a round of innocent tea-parties. This is a cover-up to conceal the real and more odious whereabouts.

At last Treasure returns, but with a cohort of chums that she has gathered en route. They all clump up the stairs. Thrilled by their outing they must now ring and report to anyone who missed it, reliving their experience repeatedly over the telephone. I don't care, as I have now callously installed the payphone. Treasure and her chums can no longer babble away my income, but they can at least fritter what remains of the day.

I ask Treasure about her homework. Does she remember her plan? The hours of homework? The tidying?

'I've done loads,' shouts Treasure. 'I do more than anyone else and you're NEVER PLEASED.' In her opinion two hours work is a mammoth achievement. And she produces work at a tremendous pace. 'I've done THREE ESSAYS. Aren't I good?' she shouts after fifteen minutes shut away in her room.

'How can you do three essays in fifteen minutes?' I know this is the wrong response. It is not positive. Naturally the Treasure is offended. But perhaps work is different now. Perhaps brains have changed and go straight into automatic precis mode, trained by years of the soundbite and tick-the-box answers.

Treasure's classmate Henry seems similarly afflicted. I discuss work schedules with his mother. 'He will not work for a whole day,' says she horrified. 'He thinks two hours is a lot!'

Her standards are obviously high, but mine have fallen. I tell her about the real world. 'Two hours is stupendous, four hours is almost superhuman, but all day is out of the question.'

196

* * *

Christmas is here again – a nervewracking time for us. Will Grandma and Treasure clash as they did last year? Will we have an anguished and desolate morning and a glum lunch? Will Treasure remain seated and in the house long enough to eat it? Will presents be criticised and rejected by Grandma? And Mrs Perez is again running away to her sister in the country.

But something has changed. Although Treasure has ordered a giant tree, she shows little interest in it. She flings on a couple of bobbles and then darts away. For the first time she no longer wishes to take over the art direction or drown the tree in sparklies, fairies, danglies and lammetta. I have to do it.

Treasure has another preoccupation – the Boyfriend. He is more thrilling than the Christmas tree and something of a raver. Naturally Treasure must be out raving with him all night and every night. We rarely see them. They are either out or asleep.

I have told the Treasure that there is one meal during the hols that she must attend, and that is Christmas lunch. Luckily the Boyfriend is also required at home for this event. Exhausted by revelling, both of them crawl to their respective homes for Christmas Day.

Feeling that guests would be vital to diffuse tension at the dinner table, I have invited Mrs B, her son and her partner. Bravely they volunteer to come. There is a tiny benefit for Mrs B. She is exhausted, poorly and overworked at present and will not have to cook a huge festive luncheon.

We have quite a pleasant meal. Treasure seems rather dazed. She bumbles through it, remains upright at table and then falls asleep again. This day is just a short blur in her holiday. No one behaves badly and the dog adores its turkey snack. Only the sound of its new squeaky rubber hedgehog grates slightly on the nerves.

Personal Bank

Treasure has opened a bank. It is the most obliging and undiscriminating bank. Any dissolute, reckless and indigent person may apply for a loan and get it, interest free and with no fixed repayment date, just as long as they are a friend of the Treasure's. Or a friend of a friend, or a passing acquaintance.

How marvellous that Treasure is altruistic and generous, but unfortunately I am not. These loans come from her pocket money, which comes from her mother.

I find that, via Treasure's bank, I have lent Alice twenty pounds. Who is this Alice person? I have only seen her once. I make enquiries. Treasure gives a glowing report.

'She's really nice. She's an old friend of Dominic's, he's known her for years and she's lovely.'

'What school is she at?'

'She's not. She's got this job. She gave it up and she's just been to India and she's really clever.'

This is a worrying recommendation. I have heard it before. 'So-and-so's really clever,' said Treasure not so

199

long ago. 'She got the highest marks for science in the whole of Sussex. Then she left school and got a job because she's so clever she can do anything.'

So-and-so was later found to be dealing in illegal substances and disappeared under a cloud. What can Alice be up to? She has a job and a mobile phone but still requires a loan from Treasure's bank. I am suspicious at once.

And the bank doesn't only loan money, it also loans goods: clothes, shoes, bongoes, a fish-tank, walkman, homework notes and now Treasure's bicycle. Most of these goods also originate from her mother. Barings would have been a more secure investment. Will she get the bicycle back? Dominic cycled off on it two days ago and has not been seen since. And where is Alice's twenty pounds? She has also disappeared from view.

Where does she live? I interrogate the Treasure further. I offer to go debt collecting. I am a large woman with a loud voice and my dog looks frightening. The two of us could go banging and barking at Alice's door and recover the loan in a flash.

Treasure is horrified. 'You're NOT to do that. She's giving it back on Saturday.'

She doesn't. Treasure reports back from her evening out demented with temper. 'She WON'T give me that money. She was in the pub buying drinks and now she says she can't afford it.'

I am outraged. So is the Treasure. But still I am not allowed to intervene. I never am. My Advisors agree with Treasure. 'Keep out of it,' they drone. 'She must deal with it herself. It's the only way she'll learn. It's not your business. Don't over-react.' Meanwhile, Treasure is losing control, her goods dispersed nationwide, her bank account dwindling.

I remember in my early youth allowing four of my pet baby mice their first tiny little walk on the lawn. They were only babies, I trusted them. For a second or two they remained in an obedient little cluster. Then they whizzed off at the speed of light in four different directions. I imagine the Treasure's possessions being dispersed in a similar way.

Still, the Treasure affects to live in hope. 'Alice has paid the money into my bank. She did it last week.' But the bank statement does not agree. Treasure rings Alice to enquire. She addresses Alice politely while clutching the phone in a vice-like grip and pacing the floor. The phone wire is twizzled into a Gordian knot. Pity it isn't Alice's neck.

I'd better not get involved. I might over-react.

Grandma knows nothing of the Bank. I am keeping it a closely guarded secret. Money-lending and borrowing are to her the eighth and ninth deadly sins. She keeps a sharp look-but for scroungers, is horrified by our extravagance and regards the Treasure as spendthrift of the decade. Our household is haemorrhaging money – on cabs, ciggies, clothes and convenience foodstuffs for Treasure.

'Turn the lights off,' bellows Grandma from her bedroom. 'You're wasting electricity.'

She at least expects value for money. If the Treasure costs a fortune to maintain, then she might at least behave properly: no smoking, sulking or swearing and respect for

201

grown-ups. Out there in the rest of the world, Grandma believes that charming adolescents are legion. But I have heard news to the contrary.

Mrs B and a friend of hers have just realised that their children have no manners. Having brought them up in a liberal way and encouraged self-expression, manners didn't really get much of a look in. Sitting at table for meals, speaking politely in between mouthfuls, eating at a moderate pace and remaining seated until everyone had finished were regarded as outmoded rules, verging on Fascism.

The friend told Mrs B that she had been away last week and hadn't seen her son for five days when he suddenly rushed in.

'I've got to go out,' he yelled. 'I'm late. You've got to take me.'

The friend was stunned. Her son is a very pleasant boy, says Mrs B. He just doesn't know how to say please or ask for anything politely.

I think she is being awfully broadminded and tolerant here. I have tried to encourage manners, but apparently with little success. I have tried not to be liberal and have aimed at civilised dinners, polite requests and pleases and thank yous, to little avail, I thought, until last night, when the Treasure voluntarily accompanied me to Hove to collect Grandma.

We all went to dinner with the two charming fellows in the flat below. Grandma had warned them earlier that the Treasure was coming. Naturally they were slightly apprehensive. They had never met Treasure before and Grandma is not one to tone down a description.

But Treasure's manners were impeccable. She ate her dinner up politely, chatted away wittily, assisted with the washing-up, admired the cats and the decor, dazzled the hosts and shocked her Grandma. The hosts now suspect Grandma of untruths. Was she describing the same granddaughter? Treasure has obviously had us fooled.

King's Cross

The Boyfriend from Hell lives in King's Cross. His street may be charming, but all approaches to it are hazardous. Only last week his sister was mugged en route to the bus station. Much of Treasure's life is spent travelling to and from this area, dodging the drunks, muggers and other pedlars of vice who crowd the pavements on her way to the Boyfriend's house.

Naturally she often asks her mother for a lift. On these occasions it is useful to have an over-protective, anxious and neurotic mother who will drive almost anywhere at any time of night to save her child from whatever may be lurking out there.

'Can I have a lift to King's Cross?' asks Treasure in an appealing way. 'I'm meeting Rosie at the bus station, then we're going to His house.'

I take her. She leaves the car. Within seconds, three large chaps appear, whooping and whistling rather crudely, apparently in pursuit of the Treasure. She ignores this hideous trio. She seems fearless – Daniel in the lions' den. But I am quaking in the car. I long for a mace spray and cudgel. Or should I just rush out and fight off these monsters with my bare hands?

I open the door, but there is Rosie. She and Treasure dawdle off to the Boyfriend's house. They are chatting away, the three hoodlums have disappeared and I must go home.

'You must let go,' say my Advisors strictly. 'She must learn to cope with danger.' Why? I would rather she didn't. I am keen for her to avoid the danger in the first place.

Treasure knows when she is on to a good thing. She may now ask for a lift whenever she wishes to visit or return from the Boyfriend's house after dark.

'Don't allow her to go,' say the Advisors. 'Just tell her she can't.' They are full of helpful suggestions. But nothing can stop Treasure from visiting Boyfriend. She would face the massed ranks of the SS, cross a five-mile snake-pit or travel the globe barefooted just to see Him for three minutes. A run-of-the-mill mother barring the front door is a mere feather in her path. She barely notices such an obstacle. Treasure has already met with far worse.

'Guess what?' she said, excited after a late night outing on foot through King's Cross. 'This man beat Dominic up and locked him in a van. Isn't that disgusting? He had no right.'

This is my chance to stress the dangers of King's Cross at 3 a.m. I do so. Treasure agrees with me. This is a turn up for the books. She has perhaps had a bit of a fright.

'What had Dominic done?'

Treasure looks a little fidgety. 'He just took some doughnuts out of this van. He took four and I took one

The Boyfriend from Hell lives in King's Cross.

and then this man came after us and made Dominic give them back and he kept hitting Dominic round the head.'

'But Dominic stole the doughnuts and so did you!' I am shocked. No wonder Treasure is unafraid of the criminal underworld. She is part of it. What luck that she avoided a smack round the head. Still the Treasure, although herself a robber, is outraged by the Doughnut Guard's behaviour.

'But he had no right to hit Dominic. And then he wouldn't let him out of the van. That is kidnapping. I told him it was. I said I'd report him. And Robert ran away so there was only me and Rosie and I kept shouting and shouting at him to let Dominic go.'

This is not the way I wish Treasure to spend Saturday nights – stealing and fighting thug-like security guards. I remark upon her good fortune. 'You're very lucky he didn't bash you as well.'

'He wouldn't bash me,' says Treasure fearlessly. 'I'm a girl.'

This is a strange outmoded idea, that all men instinctively treat women with courtesy and restraint. Where does the Treasure get it from?

'Anyway,' Treasure races on with her thrilling story. 'I couldn't leave Dominic, could I? So I just went on shouting and shouting at the man to let him out and I told him he had NO RIGHT TO DO THAT.'

How is Treasure still alive? 'It's very nice of you to stick up for Dominic, but will you please not wander about King's Cross at night. Do you know now why I ask you not to?'

'Yes.' She promises never to wander about King's Cross 207

again at night. If only Boyfriend would accompany her to and from bus-stops in a courteous way, but he does not and Treasure's outings become even more terrifying.

Now that Grandma's stays here are growing longer, she too lies shuddering in bed awaiting her beloved grandchild's safe return home. Luckily she has the odd diversion. She is enraged by the latest panty-liner advertisment. She sings the tune in a loud and mocking voice whenever she remembers it and narrates the story. She is gradually ensuring that we all hate the panty-liner advert with a frightening intensity.

She cannot ignore it. It must be seized upon and screamed at. I feel that she is setting Treasure a poor example. I am trying to encourage Treasure to remain calm whenever possible. But Grandma cannot remain calm. She is the Anxiety Queen.

Today at lunch she rakes up another worry. She feels that Treasure's new winter coat is inadequate. Earlier Treasure went out in a blinding snowstorm in the new coat but without a scarf or gloves.

'It that coat warm enough?' snaps Grandma fiercely.

'Yes.' Treasure glowers at her soup.

But Grandma doesn't believe her. 'It looks very thin to me,' says she in a menacing way. 'Is it lined?'

'Yes.' Treasure is nearing meltdown.

Quickly I step in. 'It's a very warm coat. What nice soup!' The row is on hold. Another topic must be inroduced at once. Treasure scoffs her lunch and darts away, but Grandma does not want another topic. She is tormented by an image of Treasure's delicate white chest partially exposed to the biting cold and sleet. And as the Wonderbra and pierced navel are the accessories of the moment, Treasure is obliged to reveal as much of the front, top and middle of herself as possible. Hopefully she will not do it in King's Cross.

Relay of Visitors

Treasure now has a continuous relay of visitors. Their numbers have steadily increased since Treasure moved upstairs, one floor away from her mother. How lovely that they feel at home here, but exams are on the way and whenever is Treasure to revise? She is rarely alone for more than a few minutes. I question her as she enters the kitchen.

'I'm revising,' shouts Treasure, deeply offended by my suspicions. 'Delilah's asleep and Dominic's revising in the bathroom. He's been there since nine o'clock.'

'Why doesn't he work in the living-room?'

'Because he's frightened of YOU,' snaps Treasure with a scornful stare. 'What can we have to eat?' To prove that her terrifying mother is in fact benign, the trembling visitors must be fed and cared for in a lavish way.

'Help yourself.'

Treasure wrenches open the fridge door and glares into it. It is stuffed with food.

'There's nothing here,' she sniffs. Only a hugely varied,

exotic and luxury selection is good enough for the Visitors. Treasure claws a ton of frozen dinners from the freezer.

'And then I'd like Delilah and Dominic to leave and your room tidied. And do not use the Chicken Risotto.'

Treasure sneers. Over the years she has refined her sneer and it is now crushing. 'Pffah!' she goes, the upper lip curling and nose tilted upwards as if a foul smell has just drifted along. The smell comes from my direction. She is disgusted by my failure to distribute freely every scrap of food to any visitor who cares to drop in. It smacks of capitalism.

The visitors have been here since Saturday tea-time. Off they all went for an evening out, returning for late-night snacks, stayed the night. Sunday breakfast, lunch-and tea-time have passed and now they have gone. So has the weekend.

Treasure retires to her room. One hour passes. Brring. The doorbell. It is Rosie. Treasure races breathlessly down the stairs. 'She's come to help me type out my history. Isn't that kind?' Minutes pass. Brring again. It is Chloe. I find it difficult not to raise my voice. Treasure rushes up to me pulling intense warning faces.

'Sssh,' she goes, looking terrified. I may upset the visitor. 'Her mother's kicked her out,' hisses Treasure. 'Isn't that horrible? She's got nowhere to go. Please BE NICE TO HER. Can she stay here?'

'Only for tonight.'

Treasure is shocked. 'You're so mean.' She sneers in disbelief. 'Pfffah!' The smell drifts by again. 'How can you be so nasty. Didn't you hear what I said? She's got NOWHERE TO GO.'

Despite my cruelty more and more visitors flood to the inviting penthouse for vital reasons. 'She/he's just helping me with my essay/sleeping/going in a minute/bringing my jeans back,' screams Treasure. Very occasionally a couple of evenings pass without a visitor. Treasure grows restless. She paces the house. She cannot work. Her life is a void. Ahead of her stretches a timeless wasteland of homework opportunites. Gripped by existential fear she grabs for the telephone. If she cannot see her friends within minutes at any time of the day or night, then she must, must speak to them.

Sometimes I too need to speak to the Treasure. Taking advantage of a brief hiatus between visitors, I wander upstairs for a chat.

'Go away,' moans Treasure in a tormented way. 'I need to be alone.'

Employment

Treasure has a Saturday job in the greengrocer's. It is fraught with danger. Giant spiders leap from the bananas, inebriates stagger in from the pub opposite and the till charges hundreds of pounds for potatoes. It has a will of its own. Should robbers demand money she has been wisely ordered to give it to them at once.

'Bob says just give them whatever they ask for,' says Treasure airily. What is an armed robber, after all, compared to a big hairy spider?

Treasure is dead keen on this job. She can play tapes, eat fruit by the ton, her friends can visit *and* she can earn money. The next-door butcher admires her tremendously. She wishes to work on Sunday mornings as well.

She has overlooked a major snag. What about the hours of quiet concentration required at the weekend for revision?

'I can do it there,' says she with confidence. 'It's very quiet. There's hardly any customers and I'm doing lots of maths.' Numeracy skills are required when the till malfunctions. And anyway, to the Treasure weekends are elastic. They will stretch to accomodate a job, clubbing, visiting, telephoning, fiddling about, friends staying the night *and* revision. Nothing need be omitted, except sleep.

Treasure whirls home after work on Saturday addled with exhaustion. She plunges briefly into her homework, guzzles up her dinner and then must go and visit Boyfriend. This is an imperative. She cannot rest for one moment. She is on all systems go, magically energised by her new schedule. She keeps this up for two weeks. During this stressful period, frenzy and screaming in the home intensify.

I long for the Treasure to resign, but she is amassing huge amounts of money. This is an enormous incentive to continue slaving away until she drops. She reveals the extent of her responsibilities: she must run the shop, get all her sums right, be charming to customers *and* stay awake. And Greengrocer has four small children. They like the Treasure and are keen to play about the shop while she is there, adding to her responsibilities and distractions.

On the third weekend Treasure begins to flag. Complaints have started to flood in. Mrs X was charged £240 for her vegetables. That little decimal point can make such a difference. Naturally the bill was adjusted, but then, rather unwisely, Greengrocer chased her with a large spider. There is nothing like a cheery, liberal employer to get the worst out of Treasure. I hear from my network of neighbourhood spies that the odd vile expletive entered her vocabulary and that she began to lack her usual charm.

At 2.30 p.m. on Sunday she arrives home shaking with fright. She has had to lock up, a tremendous responsibility. 'I couldn't find the fourth padlock,' she babbles. 'Bob shouldn't have made me do that, should he? He's been out all afternoon. Suppose someone breaks in? And there's £125 in the till.' Treasure and Greengrocer are not as keen on each other as they were three weeks ago.

During the week I pass by and have a chat with Greengrocer. He too is showing signs of strain. His is a tricky position. Treasure is not the most respectful of employees, but her mother is an ace customer, spending the bulk of her income on fruit.

'Don't get me wrong,' says he politely, 'she's a lovely girl, but I think I need someone full-time.'

Luckily Treasure and Greengrocer are saved by the 'flu. It strikes the next Friday and prevents Treasure from working, leaving her just enough strength to play weakly with friends.

'I don't think I want this job,' says she, after her idyllic weekend of unemployment. 'I've got too much homework.'

Can this be a breakthrough? Does the Treasure at last regard schoolwork as some sort of priority? One might expect looming exams to spur her into revising, but they do not. There is nothing like a vital, fast-approaching deadline to galvanise Treasure into play. And the nearer exams get, the less time she has to revise, the more hopeless the task and the more reason to give up and diddle about. Panic drives her into inactivity.

It is difficult for a mother to watch this process calmly. I am wont to nag and pressurise and enquire about progress. Naturally this sets the Treasure roaring and tantrumming. What else can she do? Her position is now more or less hopeless. How can she revise nine subjects in one week?

Suddenly she tries. Things are not as hopeless as they seem. There are gaps between exams, a day or so, an odd morning into which she plans to cram her revision.

We come up against the odd snag, like the lost French.

Treasure has never given a fig for French. Now and again, over the years, I have spotted some French homework, but only fleetingly. Now suddenly, one week from countdown, she is desperate to learn it, all five years' worth in seven days.

'It doesn't matter,' I say, trying to calm the Treasure, 'just do what you can.'

'It does, it does,' she screams. 'I'll fail. I'll fail everything.'

Not only her French, but all her notes, files, books, clothes, cosmetics and earthly goods are in disarray. One glance into her room would scramble the strongest of brains.

'I tried to tidy it,' weeps Treasure. 'I made more piles, but they all fell down.' She subsides onto the bed, her spirit broken.

Somewhere, beneath the myriad fallen piles, lie the French notes, vital key to success. An orderly environment must be created, then Treasure's mind may become orderly and receptive to French. This is my theory. I explain it to Treasure. Bravely, led by her mother, she enters chaos.

216   After several hours of gruelling tidying the French

notes are found. Treasure's room is immaculate. But after a day or so the chaos will return. I think I see the emergence of a pattern here. Treasure will allow the mess to grow, she will bear it for months and months, until it reaches hellish proportions, and then, on the verge of another breakdown, only hours before an exam, a holiday departure or vital event, she will call for her mother, who will help her tidy.

How could I refuse? This is an emergency. Treasure is cracking up. Naturally my Advisors often sneer at this sort of story. They spotted the pattern years ago.

'I do not wish to talk about this,' snaps Mrs Perez crossly. 'What are you doing going up there? Do *not* go up to her room.'

Only weeks ago I saw this very same problem on the telly. There was a Mother, incensed by the filth and mess in her daughter's room and forever rushing in to tidy it.

Of one accord, Oprah, the audience and I roared in American at this mother. 'Do NAT go in there. Stay OUTTA her room.' I could see this woman's mistakes clear as a bell. But will I take notice of this sensible programme? It echoes Mrs Perez' words. No wonder she is in a bate.

Stormy Romance

Treasure and the Boyfriend from Hell are in the middle of exams and their affair is volcanic. We live on a seismic fault, prey to sudden and unexpected eruptions as it staggers on. This is a nerve-racking time for us. Tomorrow loom the two most feared exams – science and French. Today we need several hours of calm preparation and respite from the emotional squalls so that Treasure may revise in a relaxed way and feel relatively pleasant.

She manages it until tea-time, but by four o'clock is bursting for an outing.

'I'm just going to meet Him and Delilah after their exam,' she says, 'I've done LOTS of work.'

Marvellous. Things are going swimmingly. Treasure is not agitated or disagreeable, the outing seems innocuous enough. I instruct her to be home by 7.30, then we can all have a lovely roast dinner at table and a calm evening, as in a normal family. Hopefully this will sustain her through tomorrow's examinations.

Vain hope. Treasure rings at 7.45 sounding dismal. 'I'm at His house,' she mumbles faintly.

'What are you doing there?' Why ask? I know what the Treasure is doing. She is conducting another tragic row and struggling to avert a terminal break-up. 'You're meant to be HERE. Your dinner's GOING COLD.' I long for her to eat properly. A famished, enfeebled, distraught and exhausted person rarely achieves academic excellence.

'I've got things to do first.' Treasure sounds weak.

'What things?'

'I can't say,' she mumbles in a toneless and deathly voice. 'There are people in the room.'

I order her to leave at once. The dog's back leg would be more responsive. What hope is there for a distant mother's instruction over a phone when the Treasure's romance is crumbling around her? I ring back and ask the parent to send her home. Still she fails to appear. An hour passes. I ring back in a fury. Treasure is still lingering there, well into auto-destruct. I order her to be at the front door in ten minutes ready for me to scoop her up in the car and take her home.

I drive to the scene of the tragedy. There must be one. I heard it in the tiny little desperate voice. I recognise it from the ninety-nine previous temporary tragedies which have jeopardised her health, sanity and future. I ring the bell and scream wildly as the Treasure appears.

'Get into the car at once. What the hell are you still doing here?' For some reason I feel unsympathetic and am having breathing difficulties.

Treasure glides calmly from His house and into the car. 'Drive away,' she snaps bossily. 'Get away from the house.'

'I will not,' I scream on pointlessly. 'Shut up or I'll get out and scream at the lot of them.'

Treasure is silent. I attempt to breathe normally and reduce blood pressure. I am, after all, about to drive a car.

At last the Treasure speaks. Staggering news. 'I finished with Him.'

'Good,' I shout cruelly. 'Perhaps you can get on with some work and eat a meal on time.' I am not convinced by the Treasure's statement.

'Oh thank you for making it worse,' says she. 'All you care about is your dinner. I have to decide what's more important. My whole relationship or YOUR DINNER and I choose MY RELATIONSHIP.'

I do not speak. My Advisors would not be pleased. I have again shrieked uselessly when I should have been calm and supportive. And I dare not speak while driving. But Treasure babbles on recklessly. 'I am a rational person,' she yells, 'and you ought to trust me. If I'm late, I'm late for a REASON.'

Something odd is going on here. Despite my cruel and heartless response and the tragic break-up, Treasure is not weeping. She is strangely composed. What's more, upon her arrival home she eats a gigantic cold roast dinner. She retires to her room, she chatters on the phone, she goes to bed. As she has exams tomorrow, must rise at dawn and will require a chauffeur, I go up to plan the morning's arrangements. But embittered by our row in the car Treasure feels impelled to criticise.

'You made a real fool of yourself at His house,' says she.

'*Everybody* heard you.'

'I don't care,' I say, 'because I never have to go there
again and neither do you.'

'Yes I do.'

What can she mean? Why should even Treasure wish to
return to within several miles of this place of torment and
the boy who has made her life hell for months on end?

'Whatever for?'

'We made up just before you came to get me.'

New College

Time for Treasure and I to inspect the new Sixth Form College. Treasure is thrilled. She must miss a morning's school, an execrable lunch, and may discard her nasty school uniform to mill about the huge local consortium meeting millions of chums.

She prepares for this outing. To investigate the temple of learning her wardrobe and make-up must be spot on. She brings a sack of equipment to the car and applies the finishing touches en route, dabbing away with powders, brushes, creams and colourings. She inspects my outfit with horror.

'You're not coming like that?'

I have my dog-walking clothes on – a selection of old and mud-spattered garments suitable for plodding across the sodden, boggy Heath. Naturally I plan to walk the dog, return home, change into something breathtakingly elegant and join her later. I reveal my plans. But Treasure is concerned with the Now. Someone may see me. She sinks low in her seat.

'Just drop me at the gates,' she snaps, cowering from public view and fearful that someone may spot her with a repellently dressed mother. 'Don't get out of the car.'

She remains in her place, suddenly anxious. 'I don't know where to go,' says she, staring at the main gates.

'Go in there,' I say. 'Look. There's Mrs B and Peter.' I bib the horn to alert them. 'You can go in with them.'

'Stop that, STOP IT. LET ME OUT.' Treasure is prepared to die on the spot. She cannot bear the shame. 'Why must you do things like that?' She is mortified. Crowds of fellow pupils are now bound to see me.

But no one has seen me, not even Mrs B and her son. Treasure is on the rack needlessly. She quickly darts from the car.

I did have plans for this short drive. I thought we might have chatted about the coming interview, about Treasure's future, her hopes and ambitions, her interests, so that she might face her future Headmaster with confidence. But she has rushed off in a bate, her pulse racing, her faced flushed, her nerves in shreds. Will this interview be a success?

Yes it is. She emerges radiant. She may go to this college, the only one she ever wanted to attend.

'What about the GCSE results?'

'Doesn't matter what I get,' says Treasure gaily. 'I can still go.' The sack of make-up obviously did the trick.

This week Treasure is sixteen. Her birthday arrangements are even more private and involve the Boyfriend. All I am required to do is make the cake and escort the Treasure shopping. But I have the 'flu. I manage the cake but must postpone the shopping outing. I need to be in peak condition to tackle Miss Selfridges. This is a horrid disappointment to the Treasure, and she already lives on a knife edge. Will the Boyfriend behave pleasantly throughout the festivities?

We hear no complaints. Treasure survives the Birthday, but only by a whisker. Soon there is another drama at the Boyfriend's house. An enraged parent has just struck him over the head with Treasure's bongoes. I must admit that I am rather thrilled. That has hopefully put paid to two sources of noise and aggravation in one go.

I would like to commend the parent but know that violence is not the answer. And my pleasure is also marred by the fact that I purchased these bongoes at considerable expense for the Treasure last Christmas. How kind to distribute her goods among the needy, but I am browned off about my shattered present.

'She had no right to do that,' snaps Treasure. 'I think you should ring and ask her for the money.'

I cannot imagine the Boyfriend's mother responding happily to such a request. The Romance is obviously taking its toll on his family too. It goes on and on, off and on, off again. Day by day our household continues to swirl up and down on an emotional big-dipper, and this is a particularly grim week.

'I'm banned from his house,' says Treasure, only slightly mollified because this is a blanket ban. 'No girls are allowed. Delilah isn't either.'

But before we know it Treasure is off round there again, till the next row, with the Boyfriend, or the parent, or the sister.

Will this romance ever end? It has teetered on the brink for months now and Grandma and I are emotionally drained. Our hopes have been raised and dashed so often.

'It's all over,' Treasure has wept. 'This is the worst day of my life.' Grandma lies tormented in bed, her heart bleeding for the Treasure. I lie awake at night as the Treasure crashes about her room in despair, phones her chums, answers the phone, invites rotas of chums round for consolation, makes midnight snacks. What a pity that since our fire there has been no insulation in my ceiling. The sound of the Treasure's clomping is therefore intensified. No one may sleep. By 3 a.m. I too am demented. I stagger to work. Treasure does not stagger to school.

The next day Rosie comes to visit with a bunch of flowers and small book of Wordsworth poetry to cheer Treasure up. What a sophisticated offering. If only Treasure could meet a pleasant, reliable, drug-free and faithful boyfriend who would turn up with flowers and poetry. In fact a couple of fellows who fit this description have tried visiting Treasure. Grandma and I are dead keen on them. They are personable, handsome, do not skulk, smoke or make the Treasure cry, but she is not impressed. She still prefers the Boyfriend from Hell.

I am sad to see that she is yet again instinctively following my footsteps by choosing unpleasant chaps, perhaps in the misguided belief that they are exciting and that love has to be a tormented state. I did this in my youth, before the Treasure's appearance. It must be a hereditary weakness. I feel that I have just conquered it, aged fifty-three. I do hope that Treasure is snappier at getting the hang of things.

225

Feeding

I realise why the dog makes me happy. It functions normally. It eats, sleeps and goes for healthy walks. Treasure does none of these things. She is not keen on habits that maintain or improve physical and mental health. It is the killer habits that she finds attractive: cigarettes, drink, lack of sleep, probably drugs, sex and raving, and now the latest and worst – lack of food.

Yet again, I blame the Boyfriend from Hell. Since her involvement with this fellow, Treasure's appetite has rather gone for a burton. She is too upset to eat, especially at meal-times. Naturally, when one is in the grip of a nerve-racking relationship, it is difficult to sit at table and eat a dinner. This is understandable, but it is still tricky to sit back and watch one's child heading for auto-destruct. I am keen to buy a tube and try force-feeding.

Sometimes Treasure can manage a few morsels while watching the telly. Or she may grab at a tiny snack while passing through the kitchen – a sliver of banana, a crumb or two of bread. Nothing in our larder pleases her any longer. She covets other peoples' foodstuffs. She begs for strange items that she has never wanted before until she spotted them in someone else's larder.

'Can we have Megapies? Micro Chickburgers? Coco-pops?' These things are now nectar to the Treasure. Had I been the one to produce them in the first place she would have spat them out in a jiffy.

I buy them. Anything to feed the Treasure up a bit. She nibbles weakly at a scrap of each later in the day. She rarely eats a speck of anything until tea-time and always does her very best to avoid breakfast. Today she cunningly sneaks from the house without any while I am on the telephone.

'I'm going to the shop,' she shouts on the way out. She rings hours later. 'I'm at Andrew's house.'

'Have you had any breakfast?'

'Yes,' lies Treasure. 'I'm eating loads.'

I speak to Andrew's mother. 'She's having coffee with sugar in,' says the mother soothingly. 'Don't worry about it.' She senses that she is speaking to a neurotic about to send her daughter straight into anorexic decline.

Mrs Perez is also nervous about my technique and brutal methods. 'Don't go on about it. You'll make her worse.' Strangely enough, the Advisors are united on this one. 'Leave her alone,' they nag. 'Don't make an issue of it. She'll eat when she's hungry.' But Treasure does not always remember when she's hungry. She is too busy going out, preparing to go out or waiting to see if she's going out. She has no time to eat. If she does have the time, she doesn't have the will to eat. There is nothing more dismal than staying in. Especially when the Boyfriend is out.

Meanwhile, Treasure is thrilled with her new twig-like shape. She swans around dressed glamourously in black, rather like a celebrity stick-insect. Her natural pallor adds to the dramatic and fragile look. It is driving Grandma into a frenzy. She quickly makes a choc cake, an apple pie and a large stew and offers them to Treasure at regular five-minute intervals throughout the day. Treasure accepts the odd speck of each.

However, her mood is tolerable. She lies on my bed chatting pleasantly. But I notice that her stomach is now cave shaped. Ignoring Mrs Perez' and everyone else's advice, I point this out to the Treasure. She is infuriated.

'I like my shape,' she roars, and rushes off to starve, but not for long. Boyfriend turns up, plus his sister, her boyfriend and a few odd wayfarers from round about.

'We're all starving,' says Treasure, grovelling in the freezer. 'What can we eat?' I am not sure whether I'm pleased or not.

Extra Tenants

Our house continues to be densely populated, especially in Treasure's premises. Visitors arrive and stay for the evening, the night, the next day, the weekend. It is difficult to keep check on the numbers of guests. A few may slide in while I am out at work or walking the dog, or while Grandma is snoozing.

Suddenly a mob of guests swarms down the stairs. Where have they come from? Who are they? I ask Treasure.

'They're my friends,' says she, astounded. As anyone in this category is of flawless character, the Treasure cannot understand my concern. She sees five innocuous chums going down the stairs, I see five large chaps, some unfamiliar, some sullen, some who have possibly eaten all my Branflakes.

I am impressed by the long-term guests' staying power. During their sejour here I have screamed very unpleasantly at the Treasure on several occasions – perhaps the smell of ciggy smoke has upset me, or the disappearance of gallons of fruit juice, or the 1 a.m. door slamming. But do they scurry out in a fright? No. They stick it out and are extra-polite. Rosie and Daisy come downstairs to offer me a cup of tea. How kind!

Some of these visitors seem almost permanent. Is this their new home? Does Chloe have another home? Do Rosie's parents know where she is? Oh yes. Rosie smiles vaguely. But she locked herself out while they were on holiday and so was unable to tidy up before their return. The parents were not pleased by the pit of filth that greeted them. Rosie's stay here continues.

And we have Dominic, the Boyfriend from Hell, in residence. This is a surprise to me. This relationship, to my knowledge, ended last week. And the week before and two days before that and twice the week before that.

'Why is HE here?' I ask the Treasure.

'Because we're getting on *really well*,' she hisses. 'We're just friends and he's giving me back my jumpers/money/ T-shirt/bongoes/bomber jacket tomorrow.' She is an optimistic child. Her faith in the Boyfriend is unshakeable. For months she has awaited the promised return of these items. She is still waiting. Meanwhile, the Boyfriend and other visitors lie about, functioning minimally. I order them to leave.

What are they doing with their lives? What about hopes, dreams and ambitions? They seem to have none. I remember a fiercesome headmistress in a school where I once worked who would stride onto the hall platform daily and address the school with a strict prayer. 'Oh Lord,' she once roared, 'let our lives not be useless.' No one ever disobeyed her. If only she were here now, Treasure and her chums would jump to it.

'What is going on up there?' I shout up to the Treasure. It is 3.30 p.m. and she has changed outfits four times and fluffed about making a final breakfast for the guests in the upstairs hotel.

'We're sleeping,' she moans. 'What's the matter?'

Again I order the visitors to leave and Treasure to get up properly and function. But she no longer knows how to. What do I want her to do? She needs suggestions. I speak to her in an alien tongue, strange words from another planet. 'Tidy,' I say. 'Read a book, do homework, go to an exhibition, Hoover, bring the dirty cups downstairs.'

Treasure looks blank. Now that she is sixteen she has entered another sphere and lives in a twilight area, involved in a collective sub-function with peers, all dazed and semi-blinded by the advent of sex. Nowadays, it doesn't merely rear its head, but rolls up in an all-enveloping way, rather steaming up the windows of Treasure's mind.

I am most disappointed. I had hoped that she might have continued to regard sex as a bizarre adult activity and buried herself in schoolwork, but I suppose the signs were evident years ago: the rabid preoccupation with Sindy dolls, the questionable relationships between Ken, Barbie and Sindy arranged by Treasure herself, the keen interest in biology and human physiology, hairstyles, shopping and boys.

'They're all like that,' says Mrs B sternly. 'I was. You must have been.'

She is wrong. I much preferred horses and never wore   231 saucy clothes. I wore no eye make-up and no shoes. I then joined CND and became rather depressed. Perhaps I am secretly jealous of Treasure's wild and thrilling youth.

I did try eye make-up once.

'What's the matter Gina?' asked Art School Headmaster rather callously. 'Someone given you a black eye?'

Headmaster has a lot to answer for: my shattered confidence, resulting drabness and the Treasure's reaction against it. She is anything but drab. And heaven knows what sort of bold things go on in the upstairs hotel. I am considering closing it down.

Illegal Pursuits

Treasure has just gone off clubbing with some chums. She was in a cheery mood and in her haste quite forgot to bring down the glasses, corkscrew and Pringles. As I am longing for a drink and crisps, I am forced to go and fetch them myself.

I notice an odd smell in the Treasure's bedroom. I recognise it at once. Someone has been smoking dope in there. Soon a passing Mr Plod will smell the fumes billowing from the Treasure's window and I, as householder and responsible grown-up, will be thrown into Holloway Prison. This is not the first time dope has been smoked in our house. I have already reprimanded and expelled the Treasure's chums on three occasions and forbidden this habit.

It happened only last week. I go out to spend the evening with friends, leaving Treasure to her studies. 'Will she have washed up?' I wonder naively to myself as I return. No. There is the sink piled with debris. And much worse. As I climb the stairs I find myself in a dense

233

fog of dope fumes. They are billowing from the Treasure's room. Naturally I run up the stairs roaring with temper.

'Who's smoking here? How dare you smoke that stuff in this house?' Treasure emerges in a flash.

'I am,' says she going pink. 'I'm sorry.' She fibs on. 'It's only one.' One spliff is apparently peanuts to Treasure. Only a truckload of crack cocaine would justify this fearsome telling off.

'Who's here?' I shout, but Treasure attempts to bar the door and protect the visiting criminals. 'Is Dominic here?'

Dominic, the Boyfriend from Hell, whose health is fast on the way down the drain, is forbidden absolutely to take any form of drug while his body teeters on the edge of total ruin. He has been warned by doctors. His mother has ordered Treasure to tell on him.

'Is Dominic smoking?'

'No,' lies Treasure. 'It's Tim.'

How many drug-crazed youths are stuffed into Treasure's chamber? Ruthlessly I push past her. I notice a drab and partially senseless mound of large boys slumped on the bed. I reprimand them brutally and order them to leave. They smile pleasantly and do so, gradually. But I am Queen Canute holding back the tide. The whole of London is awash with the stuff and they will be back laden with spliffs the minute I am absent. Naturally I am not keen on leaving Treasure alone in the house, but Grandma is poorly in Hove and I must visit her. I plan to do it while Treasure spends the night at Delilah's. Foolishly I reveal my plan one hour before leaving. There is a sudden flurry of telephoning. Treasure dawdles about the house.

How many drug-crazed youths are
stuffed into Treasure's chamber?

'When are you going to Delilah's?'

'I don't think I can be bothered,' says Treasure casually. 'We might stay here.'

'Who's we?'

'Oh, just Delilah and Dominic. And I'm just going outside to talk to Mark.'

Why Mark? He is a neighbour of the Treasure's age with whom she rarely mixes socially. And why outside? Soon they both come in, but Mark loiters by the window.

'He's looking for his friends,' says Treasure breezily. 'They're coming to his house.'

I am suspicious at once. I am about to leave my house unguarded overnight and already the Treasure's arrangements have changed and unusual visitors are posted at the windows looking out for strange men. I overhear a telephone conversation.

'Hurry up or Mark will have to leave,' hisses Treasure. She is issuing another invitation. Naturally I ask who else is coming.

'Oh only Chrissie (the Boyfriend's sister) because she's really upset. She's had a row with her boyfriend, so Dominic's bringing her over.'

I point out that numbers are swelling. We now have Delilah, Dominic, Chrissie, Andrew, Mark and the two unknown friends. Who are these friends? I suspect they are dealing in drugs. But I cannot remain here on guard. I go to visit Grandma because I must. Fortunately she is coming to stay permanently, and then I will never need leave the house again.

Treasure is still alive and coherent upon my return. The drugs squad is not lining the street. Our home has not been raided. But it only needs a tip-off from Andrea Big Bottom down the road, guardian of the street's morals, and we shall be for it.

It always seems to be boys who are the culprits. They have all mumbled apologies and stopped. 'Do you all do this at your house?' I have asked snappily.

'Mumble mumble.'

'Then DO NOT do it here.'

Presumably the minute I leave the house, they will return and start again. I cannot maintain a continual police presence to prevent this. I am now fairly certain that whenever the house is empty hordes of them nip round with sacks of illegal substances, pile in, dope themselves senseless and consume God knows what.

And here comes another surprised telly programme revealing that a huge percentage of teenagers smoke cannabis. Did anyone in the world, besides Grandma, not know this?

Grandma watches the programme with horror. 'I hope Treasure's watching this,' she moans. 'She ought to be. This will put her off.'

But Grandma is wrong. Nothing will put the Treasure off, especially not her mother or the telly. I know because I've tried.

'You are NOT to smoke dope in this house,' I have now roared at the Treasure several times. 'Tell your friends it is NOT ALLOWED.'

At first Treasure affected innocence. It wasn't her, it was X (the least popular friend). She couldn't stop him. But on this, the third time, she goes on the attack.

'Anyway,' she crows, '*your* friends do it. Y does it. So

does Z. I saw them at Z's house at Christmas. They had a huge spliff. You're a hypocrite.'

'They are fifty and grown up and may do what they want. You may not.'

But Treasure fights on, sneering and unashamed. 'Why not?' she nags. 'It's not dangerous, it's not as bad as drinking. You drink,' says she revving up. *'You're* an alcoholic.'

This is fantasy. I am unable to be an alcoholic even if I long to. Sometimes a short period of oblivion would suit me down to the ground, but one glass of anything gives me a murderous headache and no pleasure. I cannot smoke, it gives me asthma and I don't take drugs because I'm frightened. I am an almost completely drug-free parent. Even while at Art School in the sixties I avoided every known drug, shocking and irritating my friends. This may be difficult for the Treasure to believe, but it is true.

In the morning I accuse Treasure of drug-taking and Boyfriend of providing the substance.

'It wasn't him,' shouts Treasure, protecting her beloved. 'It was Pete. He's a dealer.' She is accusing the son of some respectable friends of mine round the corner. She will accuse half the street to save the Boyfriend. According to Treasure the area is littered with dealers. There is not a youth within a five-mile radius who isn't one, except for the Boyfriend, who is without stain.

'I don't care who it was. Will you tell them that if they do it once more in my house I will CALL THE POLICE.'

Treasure sneers tremendously. She has never heard such silliness. She is a modern child, knows that alcohol is a far more pernicious drug, and dope does her no harm at all.

'Yes it does,' I shout. 'It's bad for short-term memory and you are taking exams.'

Treasure only sneers again. And she has an ace card up her sleeve. 'I'm going to tell Grandma that *your friends* are drug addicts.' She knows that if she does this it will be the end of life as we know it.

These are desperate times in our house. I am KGB and Treasure is revolutionary freedom fighter, with all her friends and contacts under suspicion, and all of this must be concealed from Grandma. Whispering, eavesdropping, mystification and mendacity are rife. Everyone is suspect.

I am now growing suspicious of Treasure's visits to the Shop. At quarter to twelve at night she gallops down the stairs.

'I'm just going to the Shop,' she cries merrily, racing for the front door.

'What shop?' I scream. 'The shops are shut. It's nearly midnight.'

I hear a faint answer from half-way down the road. 'It's the all-night mini-market on blah blah . . .'

I am convinced that Treasure has found a secret source of drugs nearby. Some parents must be away for the week and this facility is now available. But the Shop is always open day and night throughout the year. There must be a continuous relay of absent parents and youth network of information to alert Treasure to the nearest available Shop. I imagine her sitting in a dark and

239

crowded fume-filled room taking all manner of illegal substances.

In the morning Treasure totters downstairs with Rosie, who has stayed the night. Treasure looks awfully peaky.

'I'm just going to the Shop,' she croaks.

'What for?' I dare to question her.

'For munchies,' snaps Treasure, glaring as if at a rebellious slave.

I remind her that our house is crammed with all sorts of snacks and an outing to the Shop is unnecessary.

Treasure's countenance darkens, her eyes glint fiercely, storm clouds gather, a monster tantrum threatens. 'I want chocs and crisps and Pepsi.' Treasure spits out her answer. 'Things that *you never buy*.' She stamps off.

'We have plenty of crisps.' I speak to her rigid, disappearing back. This behaviour only heightens my suspicions. A foul temper and ravenous appetite for snacks suggest that the Shop is indeed a mountain of dope and drugs at a nearby secret address. Will I ever know the truth?

Perhaps one day, if Treasure survives, she will come visiting me in my nursing home and chatter freely about her misspent youth and all the things she did that I knew nothing about. These gripping tales will bring a dash of excitement to my last few months of life, and luckily, I will be too old, sick and weak to shout.

Naturally I talk of my worries to the Advisors all the time. Shall I accuse the Treasure of drug-taking?

'Don't be silly,' says Mrs B strictly. 'She'll only deny it. And you telling her off isn't going to stop her.'

How sensible. If only I could be like Mrs B – laid back,

reasonable, feet on the ground. Obviously a gibbering, terrified and suspicious mother is not the best thing for Treasure. She needs a tranquil, stable presence in the home. Will I ever manage it?

Sad Parents

Treasure is now threatening to have a tattoo. Not content with the brutal navel piercing, she now wishes to mutilate herself further and forever. She reveals her new plan in the car, where we are trapped together squabbling fiercely.

'You can never get rid of them.'

'Yes you can. Nowadays you can.'

'No you can't.' /'Yes you can.' /'No you can't.'

'Anyway, what's the matter with tattoos?'

'I don't like them.'

'You don't like anything,' snaps Treasure. 'You hate piercing, you hate tattoos.' She looks rather hurt. 'Anyway, you don't know what tattoo I was going to have.'

'What?'

'A daisy chain.' Treasure looks demure. 'But I can't have one because it's too expensive.' Her life is ruled by finance, not by her mother. I have one more ace card which may dissuade her. I play it.

'You can't do modelling with a tattoo.' This is only a wild

guess. A gamble. I am not sure of my facts. Will it work? But I do know Treasure is dead keen to be a model. She is silenced.

Why must she tamper with herself? She seems generally dissatisfied with her appearance, which I think is charming. And now the dentist has contributed to her dissatisfaction. If she wants a perfect smile instead of some sideways teeth and a slight gap she may have to have a whole head X-ray, a railway brace for one year, a giant jaw-changing operation, three teeth out, a brace for another six months, and then her teeth will be straight.

I would like to slap the dentist. Treasure is now hugely dissatisfied with the minor abnormalities of her teeth. Dentist did mention casually that he thought she looked very pleasant anyway, but the Treasure is a sensitive adolescent, and to have middle teeth which are not quite in the middle is torture. Why did Dentist mention the horrific alternative?

Only one thing may put Treasure off. With a mouthful of wire, bloody craters, stitches, swellings and bruises, she may find that romance eludes her.

She is not the only one keen to despoil herself. I noticed a young fellow out shopping with his mummy in Marks and Spencer's yesterday, his face spattered with metal bobbles. How was this effected? Were the insides of his cheeks crammed with nuts and bolts? I must say it came as a frightful shock in hosiery and ought not be allowed. And there was his mother pottering about calmly. If I was her I wouldn't have bought him a single sock.

Perhaps I am intolerant. If so I am not alone. My friend Fielding reports that his daughter has come home late

243

from school with a ring in her nose. He and the wife are not thrilled. What happens when the daughter has a cold or a snotty nose? A horrid thought. My friend trudged into work the next day in despair and mentioned the nose-ring to two colleagues.

'Why did you allow it?' they asked, looking blankly at him. I have often been asked this question regarding the Treasure. It is difficult not to thump the person asking it. My friend wondered what these colleagues expected him to do. Perhaps he could have split himself into a hundred parts, guessed the date of the planned mutilation, positioned one of the parts in each piercing parlour in town and threatened to shoot the proprietor if anyone even showed his daughter a nose-ring.

His wife went to work feeling glum, because the daughter has been so vile of late, and blubbed in the office. Mrs C up the road sat weeping at her kitchen table at 1 a.m. last night, in despair over her treasures, two of whom are locked into vicious sibling rivalry.

All over Britain parents seem to be crying in their kitchens and at their desks over the grizzly behaviour of their wild and mutilated children. I see now why the elderly drone on about a golden age that is past. I am also beginning to do it. In my youth things were nothing as wild as they are now. Even Mick Jagger was relatively chubby and wore ordinary clothes. And I had bare feet in the street. In Ruislip in the sixties this was a wild thing to do. Treasure thinks it rather tame but endearing. Her mother was trying to be a rebel, in her own weedy way.

244   At least I now have something to be cheerful about.

Treasure has passed all her exams. She has As, Bs and Cs. How did she do it? I am thrilled, but Treasure is dissatisfied. Naturally she wanted more As. I must say the marking seems rather bizarre. How did she get B for French – a subject she has steadfastly ignored for years and cannot speak a word of? She has high marks for worst subjects and low marks for best ones. She is distraught. We go out for celebratory coffee and cakes, but the Treasure feels understandably dismal. And the Boyfriend is soon off to a distant university. So are Rosie and Daisy, and Chloe is off round the world. They are all two years older than the Treasure, and she will be left here alone with her dreary mother and Grandma. No wonder she is in the dumps.

Tidying

As the Treasure grows older and wilder, her life falls into disarray. Debts mount up, school work goes down the pan, diet and sleep are all to pot, and now we are losing control of the tidying. I am just about managing to keep the downstairs under control, but signs of chaos begin at the bottom of the staircase to Treasure's room. Piles of bits clog the steps and only a narrow and hazardous path remains to her premises. It is difficult to find a foothold on the landing.

These piles are waiting to be fitted into the Treasure's room, when a space has been cleared. But now her premises are larger, the problem is greater, rather like our government's road-building programme. More motorways attract more traffic – and I have made the same mistake. Treasure's enlarged premises are now log-jammed. Tidying them is a monumental task.

Once more I blame the Boyfriend from Hell. He has created emotional disorder which is reflected in Treasure's premises. She needs a fairly constant team of supporters and tidiers to help her sort out her life and surroundings.

'I can't do it,' moans Treasure in a heartrending way, drooping in the middle of her room. At any moment she may subside on to a pile. 'You've got to help me. Please.'

We start with the sock drawer. It is stuffed with four pairs of socks and forty-one odd ones. How has this happened? Then the tights. Two intact pairs, twenty-eight laddered. We still have the six years' of old school exercise books, the T-shirt drawers, the tops, the skirts, the jeans, the jumpers. Will the newly sorted sock drawer remain in order until the end? We have a Forth Bridge of tidying.

'The only way to keep a house tidy,' drones Grandma bossily, 'is to clear up as you go along.' Luckily her visits to the Treasure's premises are rare. The shock of her last visit has kept her at bay. Still I hear her ringing refrain from down in the lounge. 'You drop things on the floor, what do you expect from her?'

I can understand Treasure's reticence. I have always found housework a dreary and odious task and tend to postpone it whenever possible. Treasure has developed my postponement method into an art form. When pushed she will, inspired by Grandma, cite her mother as an example and precedent. And although my standards have improved enormously, Treasure's still lag behind.

It is difficult to catch her in a tidying mood. Depressed by the Boyfriend's callous nature, she cannot muster the energy to tidy. Any surplus energy is at once used up visiting or being visited by friends, so that the Boyfriend may be analysed, damned and blotted from the Treasure's mind.

She seems unable to tidy in the presence of peers. 247

'Why can't Delilah help you tidy? While you're talking?'

'Leave it out Mum,' drawls Treasure, wallowing in the squalor with Delilah. How do they emerge from such a pit looking and smelling wholesome?

'Ignore it,' advises Mrs B strictly. She never enters her son's room, where he often lies hidden in deep mounds of clothes and rubble. But Treasure's mounds are not purely personal. Household items and many of my vital possessions are somewhere in there – my mousse, shampoo, combs, body lotion, mascara, hairdryer, clothing, crockery, cutlery and every glass in the house. Downstairs, Grandma and I drink our Martinis out of coffee cups. I cannot ignore it. The kitchen and bathroom are emptying, their contents swallowed up in the Treasure's slum. Weeks, months and whole holidays have passed, but still she has not progressed with her tidying. If anything she has become more inert. It preys on my mind. Up there I know that mounds of damp towels still lie reeking, my possessions are possibly trampled and crushed and hygiene is questionable.

I rush up the stairs in a bate. There is Treasure lying in bed, telly on, curtains drawn, surrounded, nearly swamped by debris. Why are the people of Kent worried? They only have six waste disposal sites. We have the Treasure's bedroom.

'Pick up the bloody towels,' I roar in an odd, low growling way, snatching them up myself.

Treasure spots the contradiction at once. 'Well, if you leave it I can do it.'

I roar on, stamping about and snatching up damp and ruined items.

248

'All right, all right,' says Treasure in a relaxed way. She begins to rise from her bed rather elegantly. She has realised that some form of responsive movement is required.

'IT IS NOT ALL RIGHT,' I leave the room screaming. 'I'M SICK TO DEATH OF IT.' I know that it is now wise for me to leave this area. My blood pressure and the dog's nerves are at risk. I run downstairs for a brandy.

But upstairs something is happening. I can hear sounds of rattling crockery and rustling of plastic refuse bags. Treasure is beginning to tidy. Later she calls down stairs. 'Come and look. I've tidied.'

I look. She has tidied. I commend her and return to the living-room. It is a vile mess. But I am too exhausted and depressed to tidy. I have only strength enough to watch telly. I blame the Treasure.

My Business

Dominic the Boyfriend from Hell has made off with Treasure's bomber jacket. It is her only warm winter coat and almost new. For some reason she seems unable to retrieve it. She has tried for weeks with no success, the weather is now wet and chilly and the Treasure has a hacking cough. I threaten to go and get the jacket myself.

'You are NOT to do that,' screams Treasure hoarsely. *'It's none of your business.'*

The reason for the jacket stealing is complex. Delilah's jacket (same style) had been left in a cab in Streatham, so Delilah took the Boyfriend's jacket (same style but better quality) to replace it, so the Boyfriend took Treasure's jacket. To my mind this is not fair, nor the reasonable action of a caring partner.

But I may not step in. Now that Treasure is sixteen, hundreds of things are None of My Business: health, welfare, whereabouts, behaviour, outfits, food, bedtime, leisure activities and sex. Treasure is aided and abetted here by the bank, the medical profession and the law.

'I'm sixteen and I can do what I like,' snapped Treasure moments after her sixteenth birthday. 'I can leave home, get a job *and have sex* if I want to and *it's none of your business.*'

This morning she is poorly. She has coughed all night and now looks consumptive. She will go to school later, says she, if she feels like it. I ring the school to explain her absence. Treasure is enraged.

'How dare you do that?' she roars gruffly from her sick bed. 'It's none of your business. I do that now. I'm in the Sixth Form and *I* do it.'

Sometimes Treasure forgets that nothing is my business and chatters away about this and that, and then half way through she remembers.

'I don't want to talk about this any more,' says she, refering to a topic that she initiated herself in an unguarded moment. 'Will you just STOP talking about it. It's none of blah blah . . .'

Naturally the Advisors are on at me, the ones who know. 'You must step back,' they say. 'She is separating.'

She is across no man's land in the other trenches and we are not allowed to fraternise – unless Treasure needs money, dinner, a lift and other domestic services.

'Stop doing all that,' shout my Advisors. 'She must do it herself.' Of course I do stop. I already have, except for relapses during exams, illness and distressing periods of turmoil occasioned by the Boyfriend, when the Treasure needs support. These periods are often extensive. Naturally, when the Treasure is stress-free, I insist that she do these things herself. Only yesterday she made her own

251

lunch and did her own washing. For her this was a horrid ordeal.

'You never cook proper meals,' shouted the Treasure. 'You just lie there doing nothing.' She had not noticed that I was busily writing while lying down. My relaxed and comfortable pose rather got up her nose while she was zipping about cooking and washing. There is nothing worse, while one is slaving away, than to see another person calmly enjoying herself.

Little did she know that my pose was a pretence. I was, in fact, rigid with temper and unable to concentrate because of the Treasure stamping about fuming and grumbling and ruining the washing machine by pressing all the wrong knobs and pouring soap into the wrong slot. But I stuck at it, pretending to get on and take no notice. Because it was, after all, *none of my business*.

Holidays Alone

Treasure is crabby beyond belief. All previous crabbiness records have been surpassed. But why? She should be in a sunny mood. She is about to go on holiday without her mother, an event that she has dreamed of for years. She and Delilah are off to a small Greek island for two weeks, just them. No mothers, no friends, no chaperone. They have planned, chosen, booked and will pack alone. Treasure has visited the travel agent, bought bikinis, written lists, remembered everything, without asking her mother for the tiniest speck of help – except with the washing.

I know little of this holiday. Treasure has kindly informed me which island – Skiathos, and for how long – two weeks. That is all the information I am given. I give the Treasure £500, and she gives me the tiniest speck of information. She can't help it.

'We don't *know* the address.'

'How do you know where to go if you don't know where you're going?'

'They tell us when we get to the airport.'

I see now why this is a bargain holiday. Once the clients have paid up and are helpless in a foreign country, the travel agent can then dump them in any old self-catering cave or slum several miles from the beach or shops, without a phone or post-box in sight.

This must be why the Treasure does not ring or write the moment she arrives to give me her mystery address. Either that or she doesn't give a fig for her mother. Or she's dead, or been spirited away by wicked men, drowned while snorkelling, or flung into a Greek gaol on some trumped-up drug offence. These thoughts pass through my mind as I await news of her well-being.

Or perhaps she and Delilah have fallen out, as they often do, and Treasure has stamped off alone in the dark to a strange and dangerous disco and Delilah has omitted to report her disappearance.

Night after night I lie sweating in bed imagining these horrid probabilities. This is much more terrifying than our last hols, when Treasure and Delilah merely went off alone for the evenings. Why did I let the Treasure go? Why did I fund this escapade? Because Treasure is a big girl now, sixteen, and Delilah is eighteen, and she promised to ring and be sensible, and I, like a fool, believed her.

The days and nights pass, twelve of them, and Treasure phones. How kind. I am so relieved I forget to ask why it took her so long, and in a few short days she is home again. I have not seen or heard her for two whole weeks. Her first holiday without her mother.

Naturally I am thrilled by her return – sun-tanned, relaxed, healthy and still alive. Her plane has not crashed, nothing frightful has happened and the holiday was a roaring success. How wonderful to have her back. It is wonderful for several hours. Treasure has thoughtfully bought Grandma and me a lovely blue coffee cup and saucer each. She talks of transluscent seas, silver beaches and a dazzling social life.

'We even got jobs giving out fliers for this club and we can go back whenever we like and work there and we had free drinks in the club.' Only one nasty event cast a slight shadow over their holiday. 'This friend of ours, Rob, he got arrested – FOR NOTHING – and the police held a gun to his head for FIVE HOURS. So he came back today with us on the plane and can I have some ten p. pieces for the phone?'

Treasure must phone all her friends. We see her briefly now and then as she flits up and down the stairs. The evening passes, and then at 10.30 p.m. the visitors start to arrive.

We had forgotten all this – what it was like before the holidays, what Treasure's return would really mean – the noise, the smoke, the turmoil, and now here it is again. Within hours the larder is laid waste, air and noise pollution in the house is up one hundred per cent, the repetitive beat banned by our government shakes the house and in a flash its elderly residents are gibbering wrecks again.

I know now why I let her go.

Priorities

Treasure is late for the new school again – the Sixth Form. She has tremendous difficulty getting there on time in the mornings, or at all, doing her homework, giving it in promptly, remembering instructions and being polite to teachers and not chattering in class, but she loves it there. Who would guess? It is apparently heaven and only five minutes up the road. She has hours and even days of free time. She need only get up, fling on her own clothes instead of the hated uniform, stagger up the road and there she is. She may consume chips, fizzy-pop and vile snacks from the burger/pizza/spaghetti bars on the corner for her luncheon.

Perhaps this sudden taste of freedom and independence is rather a shock to her system. She seems exhausted by it. The less stringent the rules and time-table, the less Treasure is able to stick to them. She is an ex-prisoner unable to cope with life on the outside. Perhaps she should have remained in the previous repressive institution.

256   Today I return from my dog walk to find her still

snoozing. I am not pleased. She has ignored my eight o'clock summons and the 8.30 alarm clock. I wonder why? I ask her.

'Because I've just had my first good night's sleep for weeks and I'm *just* feeling better and I'll get up *as soon as I can*,' snaps Treasure, relaxing comfortably in bed. A rather feeble virus has recently attacked her lungs. It comes and goes in an obliging way, backs off when friends are visiting and comes roaring back in time for school.

This fits in rather well with the Treasure's priorities. She *must* play with friends, even when poorly, but *musn't* go to school feeling under the weather. She can snap out of double pneumonia in a trice for chums, but in school-time, a slight chill can knock her back for days.

The word 'registration' does not fill the Treasure with a sense of urgency. Today she has missed registration. She seems unconcerned. She will rest for a little longer, then get up in a leisurely way, and when she feels absolutely first class, stroll into school.

To speed things up a bit I drive Treasure to the chemist opposite school for her antibiotics. Returning to the car I find her chatting to Andrew, also late for school.

'Andrew needs a travel agent,' drawls Treasure. Both loll against the car in the late autumn sunshine discussing Andrew's exotic holiday plans and itinerary. Meanwhile, just across the road in the school, lessons whiz by, teachers fume and despair, work piles up and opportunities pass, wasted and gone forever. Still Treasure loiters.

Why doesn't she grab her antibiotics, swallow one down and race into school as I suggest? We even have a small carton of orange juice in the car to enable her to do this.

'I'm not taking one in the street!' She stares at me with distaste, incredulous. I have suggested an act of gross indecency. 'I'll take it in school.' She stuffs the pills into her bag where it sinks into a mire of rotting snacks and debris.

I am fed up with this. I long to grab the Treasure's arm and march her strictly into school, but she is now far too large. While she loiters about, my life is also whizzing by. I bellow at her to hurry up and roar off in the car. Presumably Treasure and Andrew will eventually drift away, aiming to hit school somewhere in the distant mid-afternoon.

Later, Treasure saunters home. She feels weak and is longing for food and a lie down. Keen to provide nourishment for my sick child, I rush around preparing dinner. I race upstairs with the tray, but Treasure cannot eat it. She is busy in the bath relaxing. Naturally she does not want to hurry her perfumed bath and hairwash for a boring old dinner. Sustenance, like registration, is not a priority.

'Coming in a minute,' says she in a languid way, as the dinner cools at her bedside.

But as I stamp downstairs in a fury I hear behind me the ring of Treasure's telephone, then a violent splashing and trampling sound. It is her, out of the bath like greased lightning and on to the telephone. She is at once vibrant, alert and sprightly. With startling efficiency she arranges a complex outing. There is nothing like a useless leisure activity to snap the Treasure back to life.

She quite exhausts herself doing this and can scarcely drag herself out of bed in the morning. She may even be late for school.

Substitute Baby

Treasure's romance with the Boyfriend from Hell has staggered on for months. She has stated on several occasions that she is in love. Being elderly, wrinkled and embittered, it is difficult for me to congratulate the Treasure in a genuine and whole-hearted way. I see the pitfalls ahead. Treasure has had a few pitfalls already, but there may be larger ones coming.

Thank goodness the Boyfriend is now away at university in the distant North, then we can at least have a few months or years of respite before the wedding. Things have been rather tempestuous round here since the romance began and Treasure is in more or less perpetual turmoil. With the Boyfriend away, turmoil can hopefully be limited to the holidays. Treasure will settle down to her work and forget about romance until Boyfriend comes back for Christmas and personal taxi service to his home in King's Cross will only be required in the holiday period.

For a few foolish days I think that we have a reprieve.

And I had forgotten the telephone. Treasure is on it relentlessly phoning Yorkshire.

'I'll pay for it,' says she, 'so it won't make any difference will it? It'll show up on your bill and you can add it up and take it off my pocket money.'

'Don't bar the phone,' she calls in a desperate way every time I leave the house. 'I've got to phone Dominic.'

Rooms must be cleared while the phone-calls take place. Grandma must leave the sitting-room, I must leave my bedroom, so that the intimate and romantic or distraught phone-calls may take place in private. Boyfriend, even from York, can cause havoc in our home.

And not only must he be phoned, but he must also be visited. Within a week of his departure, Treasure is planning a visit to Yorkshire. I find it rather galling that the Boyfriend is up there with her bomber jacket which he will not relinquish. Treasure must go shivering up there in her jean jacket to retrieve it. But will she? Boyfriend is poorly, cold and has no money. He is a Poor Student. How can she ask for her lovely warm jacket back?

Treasure plans to travel north with a fake under-sixteen railcard that she has forged in red biro. Any British Rail official would spot the forgery from a hundred yards through a rush hour crowd. I remind Treasure that diddling the railways is dishonest and a criminal offence and insist that she buy a proper student railcard. Universities do not keenly embrace potential students with a criminal record, and, even worse, if caught she might be sent home, miss her train and never reach Boyfriend.

She agrees to buy one. Grandma offers to buy it for her, then Treasure need only shell out an extra £6 for her fare.

Perhaps Grandma and I have acted unwisely. I shall not tell my Advisors the details of this latest episode. They may easily advise that Treasure be allowed to go ahead with her forgery, get arrested, ruin her future, never reach Boyfriend and return home to create weeks of purgatory for her family.

Grandma and I are not up to this. We have again gone for the easy option and protected Treasure from the world and herself. Secretly, she is still our baby.

But fortunately I also have the dog, who is an extra baby. This way Treasure escapes much of the suffocating, overprotective behaviour in which I long to indulge. I am able to displace it on to the dog, talking to it in a childish way, observing its toilet habits, cleaning up after it, feeding it, brushing its coat neatly, squeezing and cuddling it and giving it kisses.

Many friends and neighbours are sickened by this behaviour. I suspect it is getting worse as Treasure grows up. But they do not realise what a Godsend it is to Treasure. The dog and I go out walking, and I may freely chatter to other dog owners about the pets' little habits, bowels, feeding, visits to the doctor and details of treatment without embarrassing the dog in the slightest. Unlike Treasure it is not ashamed of its mother.

Naturally Mrs Perez is nauseated by all this. She is very strict on our walks. She had quite enough of this sort of drivel when her children were babies: gooing over prams, talking of baby's progress, causes of vomiting and diarrhoea. Now here I am doing it again.

'I'm not listening to this,' snaps Mrs P, striding off as another dog owner looms up. 'COME ON.'

But I cannot. I have spotted a baby bulldog. I must say 'Aaah,' and ask how old it is. Mrs P is revolted.

So is Grandma. I notice her growing rather crabby in the kitchen. Soon she expresses herself forcefully. She has never been one to repress emotions. 'Stop talking to the bloody dog,' she screams. 'That's three times you've spoken to it in five minutes. I've been counting.'

But, meanwhile, Treasure is upstairs free as a bird, in charge of her own walkies and personal habits. I feel that the dog is of enormous benefit to all of us. It is a comforting creature. There is nothing like a big, snoozing cuddly dog to play with when one has a teenage daughter and elderly mother in the house.

Debtors

Chloe is coming home from university for the Christmas holidays. Treasure is thrilled.

'Chloe's got terrible debts,' says she admiringly. 'So has Dominic.' Dominic, the Boyfriend from Hell, is also due home from his first term at university.

'Perhaps it's difficult having to organise their money.' I imagine the poor creatures away from their mothers and living on baked beans and porridge.

'Oh no,' says Treasure. 'Dominic's bought decks.'

'Bought debts? Whatever for?' I have misheard Treasure.

'No,' says Treasure dreamily. 'Decks. Record decks. He's going to be a DJ.'

'I thought he was going to be an architect.' Does his mother, or do the authorities know, I wonder, what the grant money is being spent on? Treasure hardly hears my remark. To her the Boyfriend is a saintly figure, his every thought, deed and utterance to be exalted.

'Dominic won't allow me to eat beef,' said she meekly last week. 'I might end up more of a mad cow.'

How does he get away with it? I myself have ordered her not to eat hamburgers now that British beef has been spurned by the world, but the Treasure poo-pooed my suggestion and rushed straight into McDonalds. And had I dared to liken her to a mad cow, the gates of hell would have opened.

Boyfriend, however, is always beyond reproach. Distance has only intensified the Treasure's love. She is forever running to York to visit her beloved.

'What can I take?' she asks, scrabbling in the freezer for pies, pizzas, curries and pastas, all carefully stored up by me for the coming month's supply of quick lunches. They are now off to a student hostel in York. I am finding it more and more difficult to enthuse over this relationship.

Meanwhile, in her own modest way, Treasure is also becoming a debtor. She is well into next month's pocket money, having frittered her way through this month's in just one brief week. She is becoming highly skilled at conning money out of her Grandma.

'I need some money for cough sweets,' says she, smiling sweetly at Grandma and coughing as though her little lungs will shortly collapse. Rashly Grandma hands out a fiver. She too needs cough sweets.

'I'm just going to the chemist's,' says Treasure demurely, kissing Grandma lovingly. Then she staggers out, racked by coughs. Grandma's heart bleeds. She lies in bed worrying over her beloved grandchild's health and eagerly awaiting the arrival of the cough sweets. Foolish innocent. Treasure has probably bought a packet of Malborough Lights.

Hours later, Treasure returns without the cough sweets.

'Where are the cough sweets?' roars Grandma as Treasure belts up the stairs.

'I didn't get them.' Treasure's voice disappears with her.

'Well, where's my money?'

But Treasure is gone, swallowed up by new events: phone-calls, rows with Boyfriend, bath-time. What cough sweets? What sore throat? As she relaxes in the perfumed water of her bath she can hardly hear the faint roaring of her Grandma in the distance.

In this way the Treasure's debts mount up. Soon she is penniless and desperate. 'I must have more money,' she commands. 'You've got to give me some. I don't care about next month. It's nearly Christmas, I've got to buy presents. I must have some NOW.'

But I cannot give her any. She will only fritter it on journeys to York. Two weeks is the outside limit for doing without Him. She is bankrupted by the fares and now deep in debt to all acquaintances, but still she must go. 'I cannot afford it' are four smallish words that Treasure has never been able to bring herself to use, and she cannot possibly use them now.

She rushes home from school the very next Friday, shovels her possessions and our food supplies into bags and begs to be chauffeured to Euston to catch the 5.30 train. She *must*, *must* catch it. She has no time for tea, calm packing or normal speech. In my usual weedy way, I drive her to Euston. I like to see her safely on to the big train.

Arriving at the station Treasure remembers what, in her haste, she has forgotten: pen, paper, magazine, a snack, film for the camera, chocs, a drink. Will I buy them for her? Now?

'I've got to take black-and-white film for my art homework, I've got to/ must have something to read/am starving/want a burger.'

I refuse to buy the chosen magazine. It is *More*, a vile publication crammed solid with sex. And what is her own pocket money for? We have a little squabble in front of Burger King.

'That magazine's disgusting.'

'I know,' says the Treasure, unashamed.

'What's the matter with *Mansfield Park*?' If Treasure is to read on the train, then she may read her set text. Here is a perfect chance to read it for three hours. She rejects my advice, sneering fiercely. If she cannot read filth and eat rubbish, then she will sleep and starve. Anything but cope with hours of Jane Austen and a healthy sandwich provided by her mother. Against almost unsurmountable odds Treasure seems to be fighting her way downhill, to wallow in mass culture and the seamier side of life.

Our Walk

Perhaps the Treasure's life of relentless hedonism has finally taken its toll on her body. She rings weakly at 10 p.m. from Rosie's house requesting to be brought home. And this is a Saturday night. She is very poorly, boiling hot, bright red, chest pains, dizzy spells and general vapours.

I drive her to the doctor. She has only just managed to rise sweating and shaking from her bed and totter to the car, but has cleverly retained just enough strength to be offensive to her mother in the surgery.

'Shall I come with you or do you want to go in by yourself?' I speak like a reasonable mother in a pleasant tone.

'By myself, of course,' hisses the Treasure. 'I don't know why you're here. You follow me everywhere.' She longs for the doctor to come and beckon her away and has forgotten that without the chauffeuring mother she would never have made it to the surgery.

It is difficult to be pleasant to such an invalid, who displays not the tiniest speck of gratitude, especially when

267

one has been up and down the stairs every few minutes with beverages, medicines and other requirements, and sat by the bedside for hours and when the cause of the disease is something of a mystery.

Soon Treasure comes moping out of the surgery. She possibly has glandular fever. This fits perfectly with her chosen lifestyle. It is merely an intensification of her normal behaviour – lying about in a temper feeling poorly and missing lots of school, and here she is, just beginning A-levels. Perhaps the realisation that they are hard work has rather knocked her sideways.

Our immediate future looks grim – months of a vapourish Treasure confined to the house demanding to be tenderly looked after.

Andrew rings and tells us that six of his friends have glandular fever. Mrs Perez' first aid book calls it the 'kissing disease'. Treasure is thrilled. This adds a touch of glamour and romance to her ailment.

For three days and nights the Treasure lies almost motionless in her darkened room. She does not even answer the phone. She boils and freezes, her head throbs, she feels like hell, but she does eat up her dinners. Gradually, as the week passes, she perks up, but strangely, although capable of movement, she does not wish to go out or receive visitors.

This is a novelty for us. It is years since Treasure has stayed at home for a whole week eating and sleeping normally and being polite. She is a changed creature. Perhaps this illness has given her a fright, a warning that her recent lifestyle must be reformed if she is to remain upright and function even minimally.

Luckily it is not glandular fever, but just a boring old virus. This is Treasure's second one. It could be bad luck, but I cling to my belief that when one is half-starved, exhausted, depressed and tormented by romance, the viruses tend to latch on.

Eventually Treasure emerges from her sick-room, but remains pleasant. And she is longing to go to school. This is a brand new desire. I cannot remember Treasure ever longing to go to school. She has either trudged off glumly or flitted off with a brave and rigid smile, like a soldier to a minefield. For years she has returned home grim-faced and lifeless, in need of a snack, a scream or a two-hour slump before the telly.

But now she is desperate to get back to the new school and into the swing of things. She has missed rather a lot of it to date. Boyfriend has played a major part in this sabotage. A visit to York tends to wreck the following school week. Unusually, this week's visit is suddenly cancelled.

Strangely enough, the Treasure is not dysfunctional after this cancellation. She asks to come for a walk with the dog and me. I cannot remember the last time this happened. It is very early spring. Luckily for us the sun is shining, some new swans glide about the ponds and for once the Treasure finds my dog-walking outfit amusing rather than shameful.

We have a giant cooked breakfast in a costly restaurant on the Heath. Treasure finds a fly in her mushrooms. There is great excitement at our table. Waitresses poke the fly and say that it isn't a fly. It has a black blob body and thin black legs, but Chief Waitress swears it is a mushroom root. Sulkily she gives us a new breakfast. Altogether this is a thrilling meal.

Only the dog, heartlessly tied up outside, has a rotten time. And then it has bowel problems. These are embarrassing and rather upsetting to watch after a large and rather greasy breakfast. All around us, people are strolling about in the sun trying to enjoy their Sunday morning, and there is our dog, rushing about in a strange crablike way with an anal problem. Even this does not spoil our morning. In the past Treasure would have died of shame and run off home in a bate, but this time she sticks with it, laughing merrily on a nearby bench while her oddly dressed mother deals with the dog's bottom. I feel that this shows great strength of character on the Treasure's part. She will need it.

In one and a half years she may be gone forever, off to university.

'I always advise one as far away from home as possible,' says Headmaster cheerily at Parents' Evening, imitating a thin and hungry student. Weak laughs come from the listening parents. But university is a soft option. Treasure has cleverly thought of a more frightful one – the Gap year, when she may go and do something worthwhile in a Third World war zone.

I find this difficult to contemplate. Our home will be very quiet. But we still have two springs and summers left to go. Time for a few more pleasant walks together.

Time for a few more pleasant walks together.

TREASURE
The Trials of a Teenage Terror

Gina Davidson

Treasure is thirteen years old. She is bright and well-balanced: her best friend (this week) is Rosie, her Doc Martens are in Crouch End and her school shoes are nowhere on earth. But Treasure has a problem – her mother. '"I hate you," she hisses. "You're so embarrassing . . . you spoil everything."' Her 'uncool' mother lets her party until midnight; acts as her chauffeur and her fund raiser; takes her shopping for worm-like tops and dresses – but she can't even *begin* to know what it is to be a teenager.

In this refreshingly witty and whacky collection of short fictions, some originally written for the *Guardian* and as many again published here for the first time, Gina Davidson explores the apparently insurmountable difficulties – for daughter and mother – on the rocky road to independence.

ISBN 1-85381-711-2
Humour

Virago now offers an exciting range of quality titles by both established and new authors. All of the books in this series are available from:

Little, Brown and Company (UK),
P.O. Box 11,
Falmouth,
Cornwall TR10 9EN.

Alternatively you may fax your order to the above address. Fax No. 01326 317444.

Payments can be made as follows: cheque, postal order (payable to Little, Brown and Company) or by credit cards, Visa/Access. Do not send cash or currency. UK customers and B.F.P.O.: please send a cheque or postal order (no currency) and allow £1.00 for postage and packing for the first book, plus 50p for the second book, plus 30p for each additional book up to a maximum charge of £3.00 (7 books plus).

Overseas customers including Ireland please allow £2.00 for postage and packing for the first book, plus £1.00 for the second book, plus 50p for each additional book.

NAME (Block Letters) ....

....

ADDRESS ....

....

....

☐ I enclose my remittance for ....

Number ☐☐☐☐☐☐☐☐☐☐☐☐☐☐☐☐

Card Expiry Date ☐☐☐☐